fROM

P9-BIK-039

Play Explore Discover Create

The Great Outdoors

Restoring Children's Right to Play Outside

Mary S. Rivkin

National Association for the Education of Young Children
Washington, D.C.

Photo credits: Front cover, Terri Gonzalez; back cover, Peggy Fleming.

**National Association for the Education
 of Young Children**
1509 16th Street, N.W.
Washington, DC 20036-1426
202-232-8777 or 1-800-424-2460

The National Association for the Education of Young Children (NAEYC) attempts through its publications program to provide a forum for discussion of major issues and ideas in our field. We hope to provoke thought and promote professional growth. The views expressed or implied are not necessarily those of the Association. NAEYC wishes to thank the author, who donated much time and effort to develop this book as a contribution to our profession.

Library of Congress Catalog Card Number: 95-074822
ISBN Catalog Number: 0-935989-71-4
NAEYC Order Number: 108

Editor: Carol Copple; *Book design and production:* Danielle Hudson, Penny Atkins, and Jack Zibulsky; *Copyediting:* Millie Riley; *Editorial assistance:* Anika Trahan, Jill Kaufman.

Printed in the United States of America.

Contents

Preface

This book is about the importance of children spending time outdoors. I expect that the majority of its readers, NAEYC members, are already thoroughly, even passionately, persuaded of the necessity of play for children and are conversant with the theoretical insights of Biber, Dewey, Erikson, Parten, Piaget, Smilansky, Vygotsky, and their contemporary interpreters.

It was my hope to add what I have gleaned from the writings of environmentalists, biologists, physicists, historians, and play scholars, such as Joe Frost, Robin Moore, Roger Hart, Craig Hart, and others, who write and act ardently on behalf of children's outdoor play. NAEYC's book *Developmentally Appropriate Practice in Early Childhood Programs Serving Children from Birth Through Age 8* upholds the value of outdoor play. My intent is to consolidate and convey the argument to those in a position to act upon it.

This book is directed toward all who are responsible for children in the primary grades. There is not a commonly used term for children in these grades. "School-aged" children is too broad. Whiting and Edwards describe the stages of childhood with useful terms across cultures: lap babies, knee babies, yard children, and neighborhood children.[1] Neighborhood children are this book's focus because I believe that our neighborhoods, changed by technology and society, have weakened as growth-fostering settings for children.

I hope to convince readers that children's opportunity to be outdoors is comparatively limited today and that their access should be improved. I want to persuade and motivate teachers and administrators in schools and centers, as well as park and recreation planners. Children deserve their earthly inheritance.

For Sara Stimpson Bremner—child of
meadows, woods, and waters.

Acknowledgments

I am grateful to very many people for their advice, information, criticism, and moral support. I especially thank Polly Greenberg and Carol Copple for sustained encouragement and expertise; Peter Blatchford, Kendra Biddick, Louise Chawla, Craig Hart, and Liz Prescott for constructive reviews; and Robin Moore for inspiration and ideas. Sue Humphries, Maureen Heffernan, Kibbe Turner, and Rob Prenger enlightened me with visits to children's play spaces. At the University of Maryland Baltimore County (UMBC), my department chair David Young, my colleagues Diane Lee, Tupper Webster, and Pat Scully, and the early childhood students cheered me on. My family (siblings, mother, children, and husband) were great sustainers. Thanks to all of you.

Besides using the work of many excellent photographers from NAEYC's files, I was fortunate to obtain photos and artwork for use in this book from Gustave Carlson, Ken Druse, Peggy Fleming, Steffi Graham, Sue Humphries, Dency Kane, Sam Kornhauser, and Robin Moore. Thank you for your contributions in making words and ideas visible.

No author could ask for better editorial assistance than that provided by Jack Zibulsky, Millie Riley, Danielle Hudson, Anika Trahan, Penny Atkins, Betty Nylund Barr, and Roma White. You made me feel lucky—thank you.

It would mean making some quite fundamental changes in our attitudes toward each other, if we were really to think of ourselves as indispensable elements of nature. We would surely become the environment to worry about the most. We would discover, in ourselves, the sources of wonderment and delight that we have discerned in all other manifestations of nature. Who knows, we might even acknowledge the fragility and vulnerability that always accompany high specialization in biology, and movements might start up for the protection of ourselves as valuable, endangered species. We couldn't lose.

—Lewis Thomas

Vanishing Habitats and Access

Before you read further, recall, if you will, memories of places you liked to play when you were small. You may want to sketch or describe these places on a piece of paper.

Quite possibly you thought of somewhere outdoors; many people do. Did you describe somewhere that you had privacy, independence, or things you could arrange as you wished—sticks or stones, perhaps? Could you revisit those places now? Are they still accessible to children?

Perhaps your places of delight still exist for children. It is likely, though, that they do not.

Although no person or government planned it, habitats for children, especially in industrialized countries, have been greatly altered—often destroyed—in this century, especially in recent decades. In the following pages we look at some of the reasons for this and what teachers can begin to do to improve the outdoor experiences of children.

Vanishing habitats for play

Children's access to outdoor play has evaporated like water in sunshine. It has happened so fast, along with everything else in this speed-ridden century, that we have not coped with it. If someone had said to our grandmothers, "Bet your great-grandchildren won't know where to find worms," they would not have believed it. But as I write, down in my basement, three teenagers are making music with electronic instruments. A few years ago they were hunched over Nintendo games.[1] Their main outdoor activity has been organized soccer. TV, of course, has been omnipresent. And as parents we justify these realities—better home in the basement than out in the streets, better playing supervised soccer than wandering around malls and parks. But at the same time, we are aware that children don't experience some of our deepest childhood joys—those of field and stream, rocks and vacant lots; of privacy, secrecy, and tiny things that crept across or poked out of the earth's surface.[2]

At times, too, the joy verged on transcendence. The art historian Bernard Berenson describes a moment of unity with nature with exceptional eloquence:

> This ecstasy overtook me when I was happy out of doors. Was I five or six? Certainly not seven. It was a morning in early summer. A silver haze shimmered and trembled over the lime trees. The air was laden with their fragrance. The temperature was like a caress. I remember—I need not recall—that I climbed up a tree stump and felt suddenly immersed in Itness. I did not call it by that name. I had no need for words. It and I were one.[3]

Edith Cobb cites this passage to exemplify what she called a "direct organic participation . . . in systems of nature," an event deeply connected with mental and spiritual health.[4] Possibly such experiences are vital ones.

Having been raised in a small town in houses with big, interesting yards and quiet neighborhoods, I resonate to Cobb's belief that relationships with systems of nature are essential. And historically, most children's outdoor play has been in such systems. The densely built environment of the city, however, also supports robust outdoor play. Urban play happens in parks but even more so in vacant lots and alleys, on stoops, stairwells, roofs, curbs, sidewalks, and streets.[5] Since the 19th century, streets have increasingly become vital sites of young children's activity. Close to home, linked to

© Dena Bawinkel

The delights of the outdoors are among the deepest, most passionate joys of childhood.

other streets, hard surfaced for bikes, skates, and ball play, meeting places for both sexes and all ages, and available for brief bits of time—streets powerfully attract children.[6] At the same time, largely because of cars and trucks, they are not safe places.

Traffic severely limits outdoor play

Automobiles are a chief cause of children's losing their outdoor play spaces. Roads for cars are dangerous barriers for people on foot. Roads and highways keep children isolated—from one another, from open spaces, from whatever is on the other side of the road. Little children are particularly limited because sensible parents and teachers know that their judgment and perception are no match for a car's speed and momentum and try to keep them fenced in or otherwise restrained. In cities, where for centuries and of necessity children have played in the streets, the negative effect of cars is particularly strong.

Dargan and Zeitlin write, "The coming of the automobile created a life-and-death struggle over public space . . . the automobile gradually pushed children back from the streets—accident by accident, each one resulting in an outcry of protest against the drivers, but each inexorably changing the nature of play."[7] Further, they suggest that since adults wanted cars, children were the ones restricted. Child savers wanted poor children off the streets at any rate; the advent of cars augmented their reform efforts. Dargan and Zeitlin conclude, "The children were losing the battle of the streets."[8]

Cars have another bad effect on children's freedom to be outdoors. Cars take us out of our neighborhoods to work, shop, and vacation and at the same time make us strangers in other families' neighborhoods. "It takes a village to raise a child" goes the African proverb, but in our society many of the villagers are off in their cars, and strangers have driven in. We are not easy, as we once were, about sending our children outdoors to play.

Furthermore, as Hillman and Adams point out, because we do not want children alone outside, we use our cars to provide them activities, with the adverse consequences of consuming gas and other resources, using great quantities of adult time, adding to traffic congestion, and keeping children underexercised and dependent on adults.[9]

More people, less play space

More people require more land for housing, workplaces, schools, and other services. In addition, some of the least-expensive housing, that which is typically available to young families, has the least access to good play spaces; high-rise apartment buildings create such distance between home and the outdoors that young children's safe play cannot occur, and densely inhabited streets often lack any safe play spots. What is more, in many cities the negative societal conditions of unemployment, homelessness, substance abuse, and the proliferation of guns have made public spaces such as parks unsafe for young children.[10]

Finally, our collective inability to manage the side effects of technology has meant widespread pollution of natural areas, such as beaches, streams, and lakes. Children from low-income and minority families suffer pollution disproportionately: three out of five African Americans and Hispanic Americans live in communities with toxic-waste sites, according to a study by the United Church of Christ. Lead from car exhaust, paint, and manufacturing settles and lingers in the soil in many inner cities; about 55% of poor Black children have toxically high blood-lead levels.[11]

Some days the air is dangerous to breathe, particularly for children with upper-respiratory impairments. Ultraviolet rays in sunshine are hazardous, linked to skin cancer, cataracts, and immune suppression. In the summer of 1994, the U.S. National Weather Service began providing on an experimental basis for some cities a solar risk index, predicting the amount of noontime ultraviolet-ray exposure. The scale goes from minimal risk at zero to very high risk at 10+ (see the box "Solar Risk Index").[12] New York City, for instance, had a 7 on July 5. Going outside to play is simply more complicated than it was formerly. One can foresee a time when sunscreen is seen as necessary as milk and, similarly, is provided by schools.[13]

School and work schedules limit outdoor play

Most children now have less time at home with a parent who might previously have either taken them outdoors or supervised their yard or neighborhood play.[14] Parents are much more often not at home, and children, too, are home less due to longer school days and school years. Even routine outdoor times, such as walking to and from school twice a day (Yes, some children used to walk home for lunch), are much curtailed. Many fewer children walk to school at all.[15]

Time for recess has diminished, too. "Back-to-basics" and overcrowded curriculums have eroded the time allotted to recess. Further, while no teacher would keep a child from lunch for misbehavior, many teachers keep children from going out to recess as an incentive to better behavior. Although many advocates for young children speak out against the reduction of outdoor playtime,[16] the push for a national curriculum and national standards is likely to sustain it.[17]

Humans evolved in the outdoors

Given that most of our evolution as a species occurred in the outdoors, children surely need to experience being outside. In particular, they may require being in an outdoor environment with living things. The sociobiologist Edward O. Wilson is among those who hypothesize "a human *need*, fired in the crucible of evolutionary development, for deep and intimate association with the natural environment, particularly its living biota."[18] Not only does nature supply us with material needs, but also "aesthetic, intellectual, cognitive, and even spiritual meaning and satisfaction."[19] If we hold Wilson's biophilia hypothesis against the closed environments of our schools, houses, and cars and reflect on how new in history they are, our way of life seems truly an experiment. And lacking intimate association with nature, can we still be fully human?

Wilson and others suggest that since we evolved in natural environments, technology cannot replace but only atrophy the development of our links to nature. If this is the case, children reared apart from nature are necessarily limited.[20]

Children today know less about nature

A recent study of children's knowledge of the plants and animals in their environment reveals that they know much less than older people in their culture group, although Native American children were more knowledgeable than Anglo

Solar Risk Index

The U.S. National Weather Service and the Environmental Protection Agency (EPA) predict the next day's risk of ultraviolet (UV) exposure at noontime. The risk factor is derived from satellite data on ozone, atmospheric pressure, temperature forecasts, and expected cloudiness. The index ranges roughly from 0–15, with comparative exposure levels.

Index value	Exposure level
0–2	minimal
3–4	low
5–6	moderate
7–9	high
10+	very high

Source: Environmental Protection Agency, "Experimental UV Index," press release, EPA 430-F-94-021 (June 1994).

children. The children in the study, from Anglo, Hispanic, and Native American groups and from more rural than urban areas, also reported having learned more about all wild animals, even those indigenous to their own locales, from television and school books than from direct experience. In addition to not knowing the names or characteristics of living things, children did not know cultural meanings—myths, legends, medicinal or food uses. Instead of spending time interacting with nature or with older people, hearing traditional stories, or harvesting plants and raising animals, the children had been in school or watching television. Unfortunately, too, the knowledge embedded in the nonschool, non-TV, indigenous languages vanishes along with the languages, as native speakers pass away.[21] Children, along with the rest of society, lose the chance of ever knowing certain things.

Furthermore, the development of children's perceptual abilities may suffer when so much of their experience is through TV, computers, books, and media that require but two senses. The senses of smell, touch, and taste, as well as the sense of motion through space, are powerful modes of learning. Imagine holding a sage leaf, how simultaneously soft and leathery, how pungent a smell, how easily ripped. By contrast, looking at a picture of the small greyish leaf reveals little. And since little is revealed, little is perceived.

The disappearance of nature has become so commonplace around the world that Japanese children actually have a word for it—hiraku—which means loss of grass, trees, plants, and play areas.

—Joyce St. Giermaine,
Montessori Foundation

In another intriguing study researchers asked adults what smells made them feel nostalgic. There were dramatic differences in the responses between persons born before 1950 and those born after 1960. Natural smells predominated for the older persons and manufactured smells for the younger (see the box "What Odor. . . ?"). The researchers point out that if the environmental movement is depending on nostalgia "for an unspoiled green world of childhood," it may be relying on a fast-vanishing phenomenon.[22]

Can environmental values be developed without being outdoors?

Loss of knowledge about the natural environment increases the difficulty in educating people to live more harmoniously within the natural environment. "We can distance ourselves from the land that sustains us; we cannot sever our ties to it. We can alter our environment; we cannot abuse it in irrevocable ways."[23] If children are distanced from the land, will they know enough of it to know what constitutes "irrevocable abuse"? How will they learn to value it without experiencing it, without feeling Berenson's "It and I were one"?

An "empathetic perspective on the environment" has been shown in adults as a key component of their acting responsibly toward the environment.[24] Does this empathy need to begin in childhood? In his study of elementary-age children's outdoor play, Robin Moore points to "a gaping void of understanding about the role of childhood experience in the development of environmental values" but reasons that these values "must be partly rooted in childhood environmental experience."[25] For the long-term conservation of the world, it seems reasonable that children need a strong base of first-hand knowledge.

Children are multisensory, physical beings

Accommodating children's existence as growing, moving organisms can run counter to the school's largely cognitive aims, yet a teacher cannot ignore children's liveliness. As Yi Fu Tuan says,

> The education of a child is a constant reminder that the child is nature, that its body is nature . . . . Culture shapes and represses the body, but . . . the body can be only superficially modified, not radically transformed. Throughout an individual's life it remains animal and passionate. Pure and simple happiness, intense pleasure, and the regeneration of life all depend on the natural functions of a healthy body.[26]

Animal and passionate, children—more than adults—are on the nature end of the nature–culture continuum. Schools rightly intend to pull children toward culture, but in long school days respect must be paid to the nature part of children for them to stay healthy. And nature, according to contemporary physics, is matter and energy in continual motion[27]—that is, a typical second-grader. Conceived in motion, we are born to move and learn from moving.[28] Playing outdoors is generally more active than being in the classroom.

Hyperactivity or inactivity?

It is remarkable in the late-20th century that being too active, hyperactive, or as we now shorthand it, *hyper,* is the affliction of so many young children, particularly boys.[29] Is it possibly, in part, a cultural disease that if children were not

---

Freedom to Be Gone from Home

I lived in the middle of 11 acres of apple orchard. Beginning when I was the age of a preschooler, I was allowed the freedom to be gone from home during the entire day if I chose. My mom would just pack me a lunch and tell me not to be late for dinner. I created wonderful dramatic play under the trees and on an old abandoned trailer that I used variously as a house, a vehicle, a stage for plays, and so on and so on.

The two times I hurt myself seriously as a child, both happened in full view of adults. Wouldn't you know it?!

—Betty Pettit

"What Odor Causes You to Become Nostalgic?"

Nostalgic odors for people born in the 1920s, 1930s, and 1940s

pine	Cracker Jack	hay
roses	baking bread	clover
hot chocolate	soap	petunias
fish	figs	tweed
lilies	cut grass	meatballs
manure	blueberries	split-pea soup
honeysuckle	cinnamon	fresh air
violets	ocean air	burning leaves
attics	meadows	

Nostalgic odors for people born during the 1960s and 1970s

Play-Doh	motor oil	baby aspirin
chlorine	tacos	feet
crayons	SweeTARTS	mothballs
rubber fish bait	Cocoa Puffs	exhaust
marijuana	urine	mosquito repellent
tuna casserole	garbage	factories
Downy fabric softener	Windex	nail polish
dirt	hair spray	enchiladas
smoke	plastic	candy cigarettes
airplane fuel	ferns	suntan oil
disinfectant	old socks	scented magic markers
refineries	dog waste	burning tires

Source: Reprinted by permission, from "Scenting a Generation Gap," *Harper's Magazine* 284 (March 1992): 28. ©1992 *Harper's Magazine.* Originally published in A.R. Hirsch, "Nostalgia: A Neuropsychiatric Understanding," *Advances in Consumer Research* 19 (1992): 390–95.

as confined as they are, their activity level would not seem so disruptive? If very active children were permitted more time in a safe, interesting outdoor setting, would their behavior during indoor time be more tolerable to adults? There would be less indoor behavior at least! To the extent that playing actively outdoors helps children's total development, they may gain in their capacity to engage in more formal activities. From her work on the relationship between external space and personal well-being, Anita Olds concludes that although children need to move, "many adults cannot tolerate the incessant, unpredictable activity of little bodies moving to their separate drummers."[30] Consequently, adults restrict children's movements in countless ways (line up, stand still, sit the safe way, raise your hand). Olds states,

> Indeed, it is likely that restrictions placed on learning environments (homes, schools, playgrounds) that limit opportunities for movement and active engagement contribute substantially to, if not actually cause, many so-called behavioral and learning difficulties.[31]

The freedom in outdoor play

Being outdoors can provide a fine sense of freedom. This is significant for both teachers and children.

Not only is there typically more space out-of-doors, there is less in that space to bump into, break, or lose parts of. One's body is no longer under need of tight control—its capabilities to shout, sing, leap, roll, stretch, and fling are unleashed. Outdoor voices are suddenly acceptable. One is more carefree.

The teacher can be less directive outside if the play area is physically safe. This is freeing for both the teacher and the

© Peggy Fleming

Children can be more carefree in the outdoors, where their bodies and voices do not need to be under such tight control.

children. Teachers do not have to specify behavior so much, and children can make more decisions on what to do. Here, safely, one can experiment with not pleasing the teacher. Out of her earshot, for example, children can talk about taboo subjects and use language that adults don't permit. Corsaro observed that one of the 4-year-olds' favorite activities outside was to get in the playhouse and swear a blue streak.[32]

In a study of play in a wooded area of the school grounds, Wagner observed that here children felt free to be territorial along gender lines. The girls had a clump of trees, "the girls' team," and the boys had a similar one on the other side of the woods. When they played together, they played in gender-based groups. Chasing-and-capturing games predominated, with girls chasing boys at times, and boys doing the chasing at other times.[33]

The picture of boys and girls playing chase-and-capture is familiar; probably many of us have experienced it. In classrooms today, for equity and other reasons, teachers usually try to avoid grouping children by gender. Yet numerous studies have shown that preschool and primary-school children self-segregate by sex when outside the classroom.[34] Thus, children's seizing of the chance to group themselves by gender when they are outdoors can be seen as freedom seeking: freedom, perhaps, to explore gender differences and cultural meanings, even as these change.

Corsaro suggests that acts of resistance are important for children's development and confirms his observation, citing Goffman in *Asylums*: "Our sense of being a person can come from being drawn into a wider social unit; our sense of selfhood can arise through the little ways we resist the pull."[35]

The air and sky belong to everyone— *the democracy of outdoor play*

Another kind of freedom for children, and adults, comes from being out of the owned space of schools and houses. The sky, the clouds, the rain, the wind are for everyone equally. Neither do the birds and insects belong to anyone. They lift our spirit as they slip "the surly bonds of earth."[36] Being outside expands our horizons and releases us from coziness that has turned into a feeling of cooped-up. Cabin fever is an old and quickly cured affliction yet virtually invisible in the literature on contemporary play.

Firsthand experiences in the natural world are valuable, perhaps crucial, in children's developing environmental values.

Outdoor play allows children to connect to the community

The outdoor world is where things happen. In addition to natural events, outdoors is where fire trucks scream and race, where cranes dig deep holes, where doors open into new kinds of buildings, where gas is put in cars and bike tires are pumped, where bridges cross water and boats sail below. It is where one learns to cross streets and go into stores and spend an allowance or to poke through the neighbors' intriguing curbside castoffs. Outdoors is where you sell candy and wrapping paper for your school's fund-raiser to the neighbors you are just getting to feel comfortable with. It is where you can feel brave or scared about dogs and watch how other people take care of theirs. You see how different people shoot baskets; you know which neighbors like flowers. Depending on where you live, you may be lucky enough to say "hello" to very old persons and new babies, which gives you a sense of your own place in time. The Good Humor driver becomes like a friend, always ringing his bell right in front of your door. All of these important learnings and more are in the outdoors. When children are always inside or in cars, they miss out on such experiences.

* * *

Being outdoors is important to children's development. The next four chapters focus on school and center yards, because they are increasingly a major site of children's outdoor play as well as the place where school and center staff have the most effect. The sixth chapter looks at current community efforts to enrich children's outdoor environments and the last chapter remembers our birthright and calls for restoring it for all children.

I moved to this neighborhood so I could send *my children to the stream. Now, I have to* take *my grandchildren there.*

—Agnes Welch,
Baltimore City councilwoman

The outdoors is where we meet neighbors and friends, socialize, play; it's where we experience our community.

2

Considerations in Designing Play Areas

A little pond to wade my feet in."

"A spiral slide."

"I dunno."

We asked some of the children what they wanted—the wooden playground piece hadn't been properly protected from the weather, so we had to replace it.

After answering, they went off to climb the honeysuckle shrub at the edge of the property, the one which falling from lands them on a bent-over chain-link fence or a brush pile.

A parent commented, "That tree is great. See, those long, horizontal branches make places to stand and hang onto—just the right diameter for hands, too."

The playground designer said, "Well, we can leave it there but not make it part of the site plan. We might get sued."

This actual event encapsulates significant aspects of the current thinking on playground planning. We see involving the children by talking with them and remembering what they say, observing the children and what they seem to find attractive in the environment, including the community in the planning, tapping the acquired wisdom of professionals, and attuning to the political and legal realities. Each factor needs to be present in some degree, depending on the circumstances. In the best scenario, everyone is involved— parents, teachers, and, of course, children who draw plans, help with construction, and feel responsible for the outcome. Sometimes, unfortunately, a committee, perhaps of parents and teachers, may simply pick playground items out of a catalog. In all design processes, however, being aware of current thinking is helpful. This chapter presents some guidelines for design, along with descriptions of some outstanding outdoor environments at schools.

Limitations on designs

When we walk outside and look around, having play environment improvement on our minds, we see the already done—the grown, the built, the abandoned, the happenstance. Then we wonder what we can do, considering the amount of resources on hand and the community in which the playground is sited. Almost never do we encounter something glorious, such as a woodland with a stream, a hill, a mossy glade that we can shape with some paths and clearings. Much more likely is an odd-shaped flat place, partly asphalt or concrete, partly grass, often fenced or rimmed with barriers, such as streets and buildings. Usually, too, some playground equipment is in place. Decades of study lead Joe Frost to conclude,

> American public playgrounds are perhaps the worst in the world. They are hazardous. In addition, most playgrounds are designed as though children's play needs are limited to swinging from bars and running across open spaces, as though children cannot think, symbolize, construct, or create.[1]

From these stony realities we shape our plans for children's play. How do we begin thinking about changing or designing a playground?

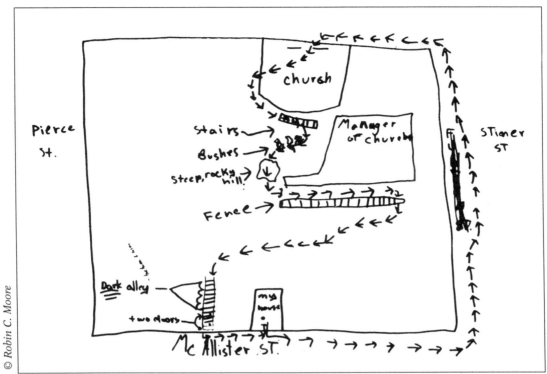

To invite children's ideas about creating play spaces, adults need to engage them in age-appropriate activities, such as walking around and mapping the area to be redesigned.

Guidelines for planning playgrounds

Designing a playground is complex. Twelve guidelines are listed here, a lot to keep in mind.

Taking an inventory. The first thing to do is survey what exists. A detailed account serves as a record of where improvement efforts began and, as well, starts the thinking about what can be. In addition, small items that ought to be saved, such as an unusual or favorite bush or wildflower, can be noted before large-scale disruptions occur. It might work to design around them. Children gain valuable mapping experience in this inventory process.

Clarifying goals for children. In their succinct and thoughtful book *Planning Environments for Young Children: Physical Space,* Kritchevsky and Prescott advise clarifying program goals so that

Children's play environments should be totally unfinished. They should be constantly changing, depending on the next group of kids who come through and make it different for the children who come after them . . . . Good children's environments are messy.

—Susan Goltsman,
playground designer

in arranging space for children's play, indoor or out, the spatial arrangement supports rather than distracts from the goals.

> For instance, one goal . . . may be to help young children learn to pay attention to teachers, not only as adults whose directions should be followed, but as warm, trustworthy sources of needed and useful play ideas, information and help. Under these circumstances, space should not encourage children to go off and manage on their own.[2]

An appropriate goal for most children might include their learning to take care of their environment—in this case the playground should provide materials for active involvement, including, for example, animals, plants, tools, trash cans, recycling bins. Clarifying and articulating program goals should be the first step in planning. Children's participation in the process is part of their development. Diverse cultural and socioeconomic groups may have different program goals—together, teachers, children, and the community negotiate the differences.

Analyzing play space. Kritchevsky and Prescott provide a scheme for looking at space from a child's play perspective. "Potential units" and "play units" are central concepts. Potential units are empty spaces bounded in some way—by a tree, an empty table, a shady spot. If play materials are added, the unit becomes useful. Play units, thus, have something for children to play with, and surrounding space. They vary in complexity (see the box "Complexity of Play Units") and variety (the kinds of activities available—running, climbing, digging, swinging, etc.). High levels of complexity and variety tend to invite longer and better play.

The number of children that a play area can accommodate is calculated by counting up the number of play places (a swing is one, a sandbox with water and equipment could have eight). Dividing the number of play places by the number of children expected to use the playground at one time yields a number that helps predict how well the playground works.[3] If

Complexity of Play Units

Simple. A play unit that has one obvious use and does not have sub-parts or a juxtaposition of materials which enable a child to manipulate or improvise. (Examples: swings, jungle gym, rocking horse, tricycle.)

Complex. A play unit with sub-parts or juxtaposition of two essentially different play materials which enable the child to manipulate or improvise. (Examples: sandbox with digging equipment, play house with supplies.) Also included in this category are single play materials and objects which encourage substantial improvisation and/or have a considerable element of unpredictability. (Examples: all art activities, such as dough or paints; a box of books; an area with animals, such as a dog, guinea pigs, or ducks.)

Super. A complex unit which has one or more additional play materials, i.e., three or more play materials juxtaposed. (Examples: sand pit with play materials and water; dough table with tools; tunnel, movable climbing boards and boxes, and large crates.)

A super unit can be likened to a large sponge which soaks up a lot of water; it accommodates the most children at one time and holds their interest longest. A complex unit is like a smaller sponge and ranks second in degree of interest and number of children it is likely to accommodate at one time. A simple unit is like a paper towel, indispensable but short-lived, and ranks third.

Source: Adapted by permission, from S. Kritchevsky and E. Prescott with L. Walling, *Planning Environments for Young Children: Physical Space,* 2nd ed. (Washington, DC: NAEYC, 1977), 11–12.

there is less than one place per child, conflict is likely; if there are two places per child, children find it easier to make choices and play constructively. Many school playgrounds provide a tiny number of defined play spaces for large numbers of children and have large areas of empty or potential play space. To help children make use of the empty space, adults can teach them group games and provide equipment and support, if needed (see suggestions in Chapter 4). Another remedy is rearranging recess schedules to reduce the number of children using the playground at one time. Adding more play places should be a priority. Children often have better luck on play-grounds after school, either in programs or on their own, simply because there are fewer children and, hence, less competition for play places.

More play places leading to more activities. Children can do almost anything outdoors that they can do indoors, and more. A useful list groups activities by the areas of development they promote (see the box "Activities for Outdoors"). Aase Eriksen further observes that one activity such as running may be primarily a physical activity, but it is also a social activity if done in a chase game and a problem-solving activity if done in a confined or object-filled space.[4]

"Zoning" the playground. While adding more play places can begin simply, thoroughly done, it is a major undertaking for a school or center. It is helpful to have a way of conceptualizing the possibilities. Guddemi and Eriksen suggest five "zones" of activities: nature, adventure play, active play, quiet learning, and quiet play.[5] Rather than concluding that space should be marked off in five distinct areas, however, thinking of zones as categories of activities is more useful. In the same way that a rug in the classroom can serve as a book-reading place at one time and as a circle-gathering area or a dancing spot at another time, a particular outdoor area can suit several purposes. The zone concept is valuable for its inclusiveness— getting us to think broadly about everything a playground can be for children. Such a playground would not only complement well-stocked, developmentally appropriate classrooms but also compensate for many of the environmental losses referred to in Chapter 1. "Quiet play" and "quiet learning" are less a concern because they can happen anywhere, but the other three categories of activities merit more discussion.

"Active play" is the activity most Americans associate with playgrounds. On large, fixed equipment children test and develop their bodies; they also experience basic physics: gravity, pendulums, inertia, the optics of being upside down. The newer, more complex structures also encourage dramatic play. Trees for climbing and hills for rolling down also provide for active play. Given that many children today lack physical fitness, increased active play is highly desirable.

"Adventure" playgrounds, where children are able to build huts, forts, and walls and to dig holes (in northern Europe also to make little fires), are almost impossible to have at American schools. First, supervision is required because children are working with tools and large pieces of wood and other materials. Supervision requires more staff, which requires more funding; lack of supervision creates liability. Second, open-ended adventure runs contrary to the preference of most American adults for the appearance of fixed order, even though as children they may have gloried in a vacant lot or other area that adults didn't value (see the box "Remembering

Activities for Outdoors

It is not possible to list all of the play activities that children engage in that would stimulate their learning and development. The following lists are therefore compilations of the activities that should be considered. No playscape could possibly support all play activities, but the aim is to create a playground that will provide settings that suggest as many activities and encourage as much learning and development as possible.

Activities that promote physical growth

sliding	cooperative games	sitting/passive activity
swinging	competitive games	observing
rocking	building/constructing	digging
climbing	walking	planting
balancing	collecting	exploring/seeking
crawling	distributing	water play
jumping	arranging	sand play
rolling/tumbling	hiding	ball play
pushing/pulling	ordering	toy play
hopping/skipping	manipulating	doll play
running	molding	drifting
throwing/catching	feeling/handling	local games

Activities that contribute to emotional growth

homemaking	music making	fantasy play
creative self-expression	group participation	ordering
solitary play	handling objects	experimenting
personal care	role-playing	responding to personal
risk taking	rebuilding/reconstructing	needs

Activities that promote social growth

cooperative games	copying	questioning/investigating
cooperative problem	cooperative projects	ordering/arranging
solving	planning	group fantasy play
listening	singing/creative noise	experimenting with
dancing	making	games
group exploring	obeying rules	interpersonal care/caring
verbal intercourse	fact learning	experimenting with
sharing	displaying/explaining	objects

Activities that promote cognitive development

listening	spatial orientation	imagining
problem solving	drawing	solitary play
observing (intergroup)	exploring	mimicking
observing (natural	experimenting (socially)	reading
processes)	creative self-expression	manipulating
using tools	rhythmic movement	describing
making things	rhythmic noise making	writing
matching, naming,	imaging/symbolizing	
identifying		

Source: Reprinted by permission, from A. Eriksen, *Playground Design: Outdoor Environments for Learning and Development* (New York: Van Nostrand Reinhold, 1985), 79–80.

Vacant Lots"). While adventure playgrounds are well established in northern Europe, Houston, Texas, appears to be the only American city where schoolyards, two anyway, have them.[6]

While a great many adults appreciate very orderly environments and value polished, errorless products, many teachers have learned to value the crude, idiosyncratic constructions that children develop on their own—whether these are the invented spellings that are a step toward conventional spelling or the ramshackle forts they may build outdoors. Such forts, after all, may lead to the adult skills of architecture, city planning, and home building. Teachers also value children's being absorbed in meaningful activities. Teachers can be effective advocates for adventure-type playgrounds.

"Nature" areas happen in some suburban and rural schoolyards. At some schools it is simply the edge of the property, the unmown and unpaved part. Or, perhaps, it is a hill too steep to mow, or a rocky patch. In some schools the area is developed, with paths established and brush and poison ivy cleared. In urban schools, nature areas require more effort to establish and protect. Politically, in an era of heightened environmental awareness, a nature area is relatively easy to establish, but maintaining it requires more resources of the school than asphalt does. If maintenance can become part of the curriculum, for instance, teaching children to care for their environment, the possibilities for success are much greater. Maintenance cannot be solely a curricular effort, however; job descriptions for school engineering staff must include upkeep of the outdoors. This will be challenging to accomplish in our era of declining budgets.

Robin Moore advises that natural areas not be overly tidied—children prefer long grass to crawl through; bushes to hide in and to pick leaves from for play food; and sticks to make fences, swords, spoons, signs, and other creations.[7] Moore's *Plants for Play* provides detailed, climate- and terrain-specific information on which plants support various aspects of children's play—climbing, swinging, hiding, or using for props (pinecones and acorns, for example)—which plants aid aesthetic and sensory development, and which plants or parts of them are toxic.[8] The information helps teachers provide plants that children can actively use in their play. An additional benefit is providing plant life that enables children to develop a lasting appreciation of vegetation as a part of the ecosystem, a survival skill for their adulthood on an interdependent planet.[9]

On large, fixed equipment children develop their bodies and experience basic physics—gravity, pendulums, inertia, the optics of being upside down.

Remembering Vacant Lots

When I was growing up, every neighborhood had a vacant lot some-where where children gathered—building forts, picking berries, digging to China, and just hanging out. I regret that children do not have that now.

—Nancy Alexander

We had some woods near my home and elementary school . . . . There were trails all through them and we made houses in certain areas. And, of course, there was the proverbial "dead man's cliff"—what was prob-ably only a small incline, but, of course, the story was that someone had fallen off and been killed. There are some wooded areas near us now, but I would never let my children go there to ramble and play. Come to think of it, I'm not sure that my mother knew about me playing in the woods so much back then. It's amazing more kids aren't or weren't hurt when I remember some of the things we did! Going through big sewer pipes, play-ing in woods, jumping on the trampoline of someone who wasn't home, and so on!

—Janet Chapman

We all have these lovely memories of magnificent adventures in what . . . were relatively safe play areas, and then we develop sanitized out-door areas at our preschools and lesson plans to go with [them]. Any ideas of how we can capture the best of both worlds for this generation . . . ?

—Jenny Bilmes

Some nature areas focus on supporting wildlife, the goal of the "wildlife habitat" movement, rather than creating play areas for children. Government departments of natural re-sources (forestry, fish, game, agriculture), however, and orga-nizations, such as the National Wildlife Federation, encourage schools to deliberately attract small wildlife to their nature areas for the benefit of both the wildlife and children. A single habitat such as a pond, attracting frogs, toads, small fish, salamanders, turtles, crayfish, lizards, and dragonflies, also fascinates, informs, and pleases children. Care is necessary for the protection of both children and animals in these habitats. Christina Rossetti, living in the 19th century before natural play habitats shrank so drastically, had to promise a frog, as her verse goes, "I'll not pelt you with stick and stone"—reminding us, too, that children's cruelty to small animals occasionally occurs.

The importance of providing access to nature cannot be overestimated. Prescott summarizes two decades of research on physical environments for children, observing that children need a "sense of being in nature."

> Natural things have three qualities that are unique: their unending diversity, the fact that they are not created by people, and their feeling of timelessness—the mountain, river, or trees described in fairy tales and myths still exist today. These qualities would seem to show children a different reality from that of man-made articles.[10]

Schools and centers lacking natural areas shortchange children.

Providing for loose parts. The term "loose parts" captures what every early childhood teacher knows to the bone: you have to have lots of gear to make a go of it. In 1971 Simon Nicholson wrote "How Not to Cheat Children," giving his theory of loose parts: that children's inventiveness and ability to discover are "directly proportional to the number and kind of variables" in their environment.[11] In built, compared to natural (twiggy, stony, mossy) playgrounds, materials for play are needed. Expanding

"Children's drive to create private spaces is so deep that many urban children find opportunities despite all the obstacles."—David Sobel, **Children's Special Places.**

A cavernous forsythia,
our hideout, crowded the fence.
Among its roots we knelt
building a miniature farm
of bricks and sticks and stones,
stocking the dirt cellar
with grass and medicine bottles
filled with berries and honey.
We wrote our farm's story
on scrolls we buried beside it.

—Pamela Warfield, "Back Yard"

on the theory, Leland G. Shaw suggests several categories of loose parts (see the box "Categories of Loose Parts"). Storage is key in a well-equipped playground; it must be provided to prevent attractive or small items from "walking off" and conveniently located for the playground supervisors.[12]

Considering local climate and weather. Schools in which children have access to the outdoors have planned for the vagaries of weather. In the rainy Pacific Northwest, a school has a hugh roofed pavilion; at Coombes School in England, the nature trails are paved so to be always available. Seven Oaks School in Maryland ensures maximum use of the three new ponds and woodland trail, with class-size supplies of rubber boots. To facilitate snow play, schools can make hills available for sledding or even build a hill with fill dirt, perhaps from excavating a pond.

Making activities and equipment accessible. America's broadening of civil rights to include the education of children with disabilities (Public Laws 94-142 and 99-457) applies on the playground as well as in the school. The Americans with Disabilities Act of 1990 specifically requires that public facilities be accessible to all. Playgrounds are excellent places for including children with varying abilities because play's attraction for children can reduce the impact of differences and disabilities. Furthermore, the developmental benefits of outdoor play need to be available to all children. Several resources and accessibility guidelines for play equipment areas

© Marietta Lynch

Children can have fun playing outdoors in any kind of weather if schools plan their playgrounds accordingly.

Categories of Loose Parts

Type	Examples	Comments
playground equipment	pulleys, teeter-totters, merry-go-rounds	first items to break
large, movable, non-objective pieces	huge blocks, foam chunks, tires	encouraging cooperation and creative enclosures
sand	sand pit or box	needing items for digging, molding, etc.
water	flowing streams being better than standing water	possibly needing pump arrangement
"building materials"	boards, blankets, cardboard boxes	turning into huts, cages, caves, rocket ships
tools	hammers, saws, nails, screws, vises	requiring instruction and supervision
containers	buckets, cups, pots, pans, watering cans, strainers, etc.	leading to sand and water play and watering of plants
wheel toys	bikes, trikes, wagons, carts	needing pathway systems
toys	balls, games, jump ropes, dolls	subject to new cultural input—TV shows, movies, etc.
natural items	sticks, leaves, rocks, moss, grasses, flowers, insects, pinecones, seeds, pods, berries	the original loose parts

Source: Adapted by permission, from L.G. Shaw, "Designing Playgrounds for Able and Disabled Children," in *Spaces for Children: The Built Environment and Child Development,* eds. C.S. Weinstein and T. G. David (New York: Plenum, 1987), 205–10.

Life is always a rich and steady time when you are waiting for something to happen or to hatch.

—E.B. White,
Charlotte's Web

are given in Appendix C. Each playground needs to conform to its particular jurisdiction's codes as well as to the Uniform Federal Accessibility Standards.

Ensuring staff involvement in planning. Most playgrounds are not designed, or even contributed to by teachers, particularly in the public schools; they tend to just be there, outside. However, as we become more aware of how much children need and benefit from outdoor play and learning and if neighborhood conditions for children's play continue to decline, teachers and principals may engage in more active roles. They know their children, know the value of play, and know what works for curriculum. As Dempsey and Frost state, "the playground must not be relegated to an afterthought in either the design or the funding of educational environments."[13]

Reclaiming the playground as a legitimate site for education is an enormous task. Teachers and administrators working with parents and the broader community ensures good quality and lasting support. At Gullet Elementary School in Austin, Texas, principal Diane Crowe joined with teachers and community supporters to focus the school's attention and its schoolyard on living things: plants and animals abound. Safe enclosures, a compost pile, gardens, a greenhouse, and a goldfish pond create an environment that supports the more than 100 animals, not counting the fish. The children own the animals and support them by raising money with recycling and other activities.[14] The playground and the school building are contiguous in their philosophy and effect. The school is unique in its district, showing the substantial effect that an individual principal and staff can exert in incorporating the outdoor environment.[15]

Engaging children in planning. Children will play wherever they can, with whatever is at hand. If responsible adults seriously consider children as partners in designing their own play environment, however, the result can be more varied and valued. A long-time observer of children's interactions with their environments, Roger Hart notes that children have natural capabilities and interests in planning their environ-

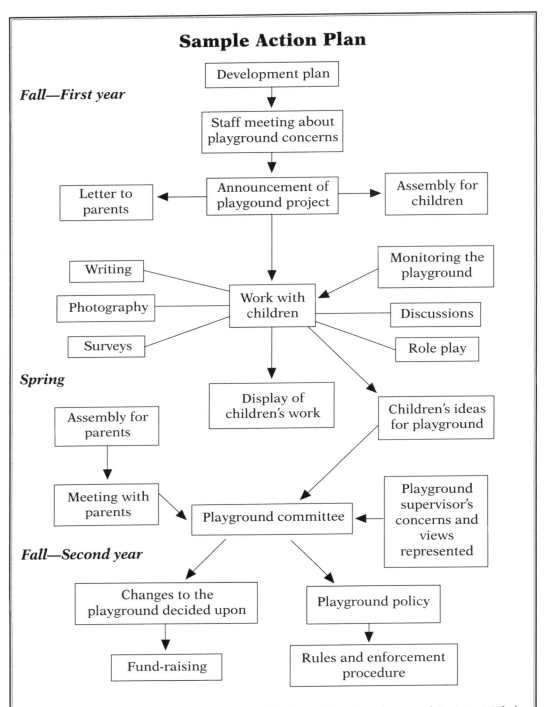

Sample Action Plan

Fall—First year

Development plan

↓

Staff meeting about playground concerns

↓

Letter to parents ← Announcement of playgound project → Assembly for children

↓

Writing

Photography

Surveys

Monitoring the playground

Discussions

Role play

→ Work with children ←

Spring

Display of children's work

Children's ideas for playground

Assembly for parents

↓

Meeting with parents

→ Playground committee ← Playground supervisor's concerns and views represented

Fall—Second year

Changes to the playground decided upon

Playground policy

↓

Fund-raising

↓

Rules and enforcement procedure

Source: Adapted by permission, from C. Ross and A. Ryan, "Changing Playground Society: A Whole-School Approach," in *Breaktime and the School: Understanding and Changing Playground Behaviour*, eds. P. Blatchford and S. Sharp (New York: Routledge, 1994), 181. © Peter Blatchford and Sonia Sharp.

ment and, from at least age 3, they move materials around to create spaces for themselves.[16] Furthermore, he believes that engaging children provides them practice in democratic processes. Hart and others, however, caution against merely putting children on adult committees (with the danger of condescension or slighting) but recommend inviting children's ideas through age-appropriate means, such as map making, creating drawings, asking open-ended questions, and taking walks around the area being planned.[17] Two playgrounds that involved children and the community in their planning and implementation are exemplars of this process: the Washington School Environmental Yard in Berkeley, California, and the Fountain Elementary School playground in Grand Rapids, Michigan.

In planning for the Washington School Environmental Yard (pictured in "Places for Play" following page 42), the playground of a public school, every child in the school was asked what was good and what should be changed about the playground; some children drew designs or built models of improvements. Children's ideas led to the transformation of an acre and a half of asphalt into a playground containing two ponds, a small stream and waterfall, woodland, meadows, clubhouses, gardens, sand, learning stations, climbing structures, swings, and slides. Half of the playground remained asphalt for such games as jump rope and basketball. Finishing the project took seven years and involved university–school collaboration, with community cooperation.[18]

For the Fountain Elementary School, children listed activities they wanted to do on the playground and designed structures and areas that would accommodate these activities. The playground designer coordinated the children's ideas, using child development as well as landscape design theory.[19]

Making an overall action plan. Because changing a playground is a long-term process, an action plan guides the process.[20] Ross and Ryan suggest that the plan can be made even after the process of change has started, in order to see where the gaps are and what needs to be done (see the box "Sample Action Plan").

Providing play leaders. An important part of improving children's outdoor play is having trained and interested adults available to monitor materials, teach games, facilitate groups, and oversee the use of tools and equipment. Joe Frost writes, "Even limited training in play and play leadership can lead to significant changes in teacher and caregiver behavior and child play behavior during outdoor play."[21] Part of planning a good playground is providing the personnel to staff it.

Commit to maintaining the playground

The playground literature is replete with examples of wonderful playgrounds that were not maintained and, hence, did not last. It is ironic that the most enduring playgrounds are those with huge metal structures embedded in concrete that, though thoughtfully installed for earlier generations, are the most dangerous. But even a playground built today, conforming to all the safety standards, like a school building, will not last without maintenance. Maintenance must be built into budgets and staff responsibilities.

* * *

In planning playgrounds, teachers and principals start with a real and imperfect space. By defining their own goals, incorporating children's ideas and efforts, enlisting community and expert support, and following principles of development for all children, they are able to transform these spaces into areas of delight and learning. An unswerving commitment to maintenance is necessary to ensure that the play area lasts and evolves as new interests develop. The next chapter discusses further some examples of wonderful school playgrounds.

3

Great
School Grounds

At this point, take some time to envision a wonderful play area for your school or center. If you already have an acceptable play environment, what would you like to add? Take a piece of paper and sketch your ideas.

The play areas about to be described and those glimpsed in the previous chapter are ones that have inspired me. My list is, of course, too short! If your playground is remarkable, write about it, share it in some way—to inspire and guide improving playgrounds. I would be interested in hearing from you. To contact me, see information in Appendix E.

None of the three schoolyards described in this chapter include every feature that was suggested as desirable in the previous chapter. Yet each of them, by being creatively linked to its specific surroundings, offers much to the children who use it.

Schoolyards that are linked to their surroundings

One very useful function that schoolyards can serve is in helping make children's neighborhoods more meaningful to them. Just as we give children dolls and stoves so that they can explore aspects of their home life in play, we can give them a schoolyard that reflects the neighborhood. As John Dewey believed, school should provide a simplified model of existing social life.[1] A description follows of three schools in very different neighborhoods that illustrate this principle.

Coombes Infant and Nursery School in Britain, comparable to U.S. elementary schools in the ages of children enrolled, sits on the ridge of a rolling slope of farmland and trees on the outskirts of a village about an hour's drive from London. Immediately surrounding the unremarkable one-story building is a richly educative natural environment. An asphalt play space (pictured in "Places for Play" following page 42) adjoins the school and is painted with math designs, such as a compass and hundreds table. Long logs at the side allow climbing and familiarity with trees. Two wooden row boats offer dramatic play places. Thickly planted areas border the asphalt, harboring birds and other small wildlife. Nature trails, hard-surfaced for all-weather use, weave through the bushes and trees. At various spots one finds ponds with lilies, frogs, and fish; and also groves of fruit and nut trees, gardens, a sheep pen, an arboretum, and compost piles. Nooks for refuge and quiet play are everywhere.

Everything has been developed by the principal Sue Humphries, the teaching staff, and the children, with community support, over more than two decades. The school considers the grounds essential to its curriculum. The nationally mandated curriculum is not bypassed by the school's curriculum but is enacted and amplified constructively and imaginatively.[2] Inside, strongly constructed books written by children and teachers document various projects that have contributed to the development of the environment. Each year the school undertakes new projects so that in their belief "every child who attends the school will have a dynamic and positive effect on the landscape by virtue of the work in which he or she will be engaged throughout the year."[3] Every child, every year, plants at least one tree.

Each project improves the environment—preserving its history by restoring part of it to an earlier, forested condition, making nature more accessible for study (e.g., four ponds accommodate more children than three ponds) and attracting more wildlife that can be studied. The box "Maze Planting Project" describes a 1992–93 project of the school, showing the level of ongoing commitment to the landscape, the attention to the multiple roles of plants (supporting butterflies, birds, the art curriculum, and play), the connection to larger efforts (International Year of the Maze), *and* the appreciation of play—this is a project for children who seek mystery in their play. The purpose at Coombes is farseeing:

> By encouraging children to start with the conservation and improvement of the local and familiar, we hope that they will move on to more global, or long-range issues in a natural progression of thought, interest, concern and action.[4]

Children who learn to cherish their own spot of ground may have the inclination to cherish more remote ground, such as a distant rain forest.

Adjacent to the school lives a full-time caretaker whose position is essential to the maintenance of this complex environment. The school does not look like a model farm—it looks like a place where things are being started and worked on. It looks very alive. Humphries and Rowe, who are the school's head and assistant head, describe Coombes more fully,[5] and Blatchford further details its merits, concluding with the judgment that

> On a continuum of efforts to make the playground an educational resource, it is the top end of a scale on which others might judge their own efforts.[6]

The rich natural environment of Coombes, its link to rural origins, and the focus on children's caring for this natural

---

Maze Planting Project at Coombes School

In 1991, the International Year of the Maze, the children had helped to design and create a large turf maze in the grounds. . . .

• This year [1992-93] we decided to plant the turf banks with around 400 willow wands (*Salix viminalis*, *Salix cinerea*, and *Salix fragilis*).

• The planting was multi-purpose: the habitat value of willows is high as they provide moth and butterfly food as well as nesting sites. They are also recognized for their bank holding characteristic.

• The species were mixed in order to provide materials suitable for weaving, and to give a mixed color effect on the walls of the maze.

• The willows will add to the height of the maze walls and make it a more generally mysterious place to play in.

• Success rate has been lower than that of the planted willow bank, and further planting is needed in the autumn.

Source: Reprinted by permission, from Coombes County Infant and Nursery School, "1993 Berkshire Environmental Action Award" (Coombes School, Reading, Berks, UK, photocopy), n.p.

environment contrast with the use of outdoor space by a New York City school, described next. Here, too, the curriculum relates to the outdoor play area, but the focus in this urban schoolyard is on children expressing themselves in a built environment.

The Creative Playground/Outdoor Learning Center is a recent project at P.S. 197 in New York City. Previously an unused, unlovely, chain-link-fenced 44-by-102-foot patch of asphalt adjoined to an ordinary big-city school, like Coombes, it reflects its surroundings, but very different ones. Models of neighborhood landmarks are the playground equipment—the Apollo Theater, a brownstone house, a police- and fire-station site, the 135th Street railroad bridge (over a blue poured-rubber river). Raised beds of fresh, unpolluted soil for roses and vegetables, a trellis, and benches form the garden area; the theater provides a stage for group performances. In a description of the area, Rosario Mora states that the concept guiding the design was a "playground as stage set," a place that children could reinterpret in numerous ways at many levels of creativity and free expression.[7] Like Coombes, the P.S. 197 playground links curriculum and play, and K–6 children use it all day. Committees of children also help maintain the playground.

A coalition of several groups created the playground: the Harlem Hospital Injury Prevention Program, the New York City Department of Parks and Department of Health, and the City Volunteer Corps. Dr. Barbara Barlow, chief of pediatrics at Harlem Hospital, wanted to make safer playgrounds to prevent children from having to come to the hospital.[8] Poured rubber on all of the play surfaces except the garden is the outstanding safety feature, accounting for more than 25% of the total project cost.[9] The Harlem Hospital has a presence on the playground—a crawl-through tube in which "You go in sick and come out well," according to the designer Sam Kornhauser.[10]

Sde Eliyahu, a kibbutz in northern Israel, shows another kind of playground that reflects its setting. This farm kibbutz near the Jordanian border provides its young children at play with materials that allow them to replicate the settlement conditions of the surroundings. Along with some traditional playground equipment, there are large quantities of leftovers from adult building activities—wire, wheels, boxes, pipes, tires, for instance. For a week at a time, children may stake out space in the playyard to work as individuals or in small groups to construct their structures for play. Their activity echoes kibbutz history—bringing themselves and resources to the land and working to make something productive. To an American observer the abundance and nature of the materials offered to the children might elicit safety concerns. What they underscore is the fact that playgrounds reflect their cultural context. These materials in the Sde Eliyahu playground—the epitome of "loose parts"—are a far cry from the plastic, soft-surfaced, lightweight toys that fill many American sandboxes. These kibbutz materials link children to adult activities, emphasizing the importance of children to a relatively small and historically beleaguered people.[11]

In each of the playground examples, adults had a vision for the children—creating safe, meaningful places for their play. When children's play spaces are related to their surroundings, one might argue, children are better prepared for living in this mobile, restless world of ours. The unconscious rootedness that has characterized most human existence is vanishing;

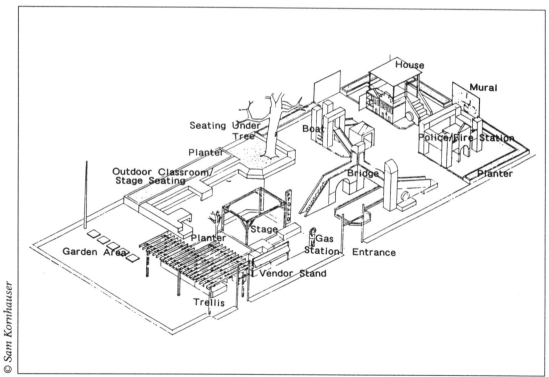

The Creative Playground/Outdoor Learning Center at P.S. 197 in New York City is illustrated in this conceptual axonometric drawing, showing the overall space layout and volume of the structures. New ideas and details were incorporated during the building process.

Great School Grounds—**39**

deliberate promotion of children's affiliation with the places where they live, perhaps, can compensate.

Gardens, wildlife habitats, and other nature-based enhancements

Reflecting the resurgence in environmentalism in the 1990s, efforts to bring gardening and conservation to children's school grounds are flourishing in many places. Reasons for these efforts include simple beautification, providing outdoor laboratories for school subjects, restoring habitat for diverse wild-plant and small-animal species, and fostering qualities of nurturing and stewardship in children. The issue of stewardship seems particularly intense as director Bill Lucas of Learning Through Landscapes in Great Britain argues, because "the hidden curriculum of the school ground" influences children in subtle, long-lasting ways. From a study in which hundreds of British children were interviewed regarding their interpretation of their school grounds, Lucas concluded the following:

> Children "read" school grounds as they read any external environment. They see a set of "symbols" from which they deduce what it is they are supposed to be doing or feeling. So a well-tended pond may be read as an indicator that the school cares, while the total absence of seating or shelter is likely to suggest that a school places little value on its pupils. Pupils deduce a cultural context in which their activities take place .... Tawdry and second-rate grounds ... demonstrate an uncaring attitude to the very children on whom the survival of the planet depends.[12]

In other words, we need to expand our thinking beyond marigolds in the spring. Such expanded thinking is reflected by the projects discussed below.

Learning Through Landscapes *(LTL)* is a highly successful national organization in Britain that was founded in 1990, following research about school grounds. It aims to persuade teachers of the educational value of schoolyards, using publications, videos, curriculum guides, and books (see "Learning through Landscapes" in Appendix A), and a national telephone service, aided by a press campaign. By 1993 one-third of all schools in Britain had joined what LTL's director describes as a "movement that has reasserted the value of experiential learning outdoors, the power of landscape, and the need to reconnect a generation of young people to the soil, to share with them the value of growing things."[13] LTL helps individual schools develop and implement their own plans, creating a wide variety of schoolyards.

> An LTL school might have any one or more of these features in its grounds: an arboretum, a butterfly garden, a checkerboard garden, a corn field, a distinctively designed fence, a formal garden, a hen house, large numbers of attractive seats, a math trail, a maze, an orchard, a pond, a recycling center, a sculpture, a sensory garden, a sheep paddock, a vegetable garden, a weather station, a wildflower meadow, a windmill.[14]

Although, in these examples, play is not a focus, Lucas believes that the "quality of play improves" when the children experience a visibly caring environment.[15]

Although LTL schools differ according to circumstances, Lucas states that five basics can make the schoolyard "child-centered." There should be trees for shade, shelter, and structure. Seating distinguishes spaces for sitting, thinking, watching, studying, and reading. Native plants are vital—it is children's birthright to know plants indigenous to their location. Water comforts, fascinates, and instructs. Accessibility for all children benefits all children. For example, children in wheelchairs or leg braces can more easily use elevated water tables and planter beds.[16]

Some advocates for children's play observe that the creation of conservation areas and gardens can work against play because such areas usually restrict what can occur there.[17] May one pick up pinecones along the nature trail? Furthermore, in a small play area, perhaps space should not be limited to a "nature preserve"— such areas need to be fully available to children. Most of us would agree, however, that allowing many acres of suburban and rural schools, in particular, to be ungrassed fosters a more diverse habitat. Urban schools can "de-asphalt."

At one time or another in our lives, nature touches you . . . and me . . . and all of us in some personal, special way. Her immense mystery opens to us a little of its stunning purity, reminding us of a Life that is greater than the little affairs of man. I have never underestimated the value of such moments of touching and entering into nature. I have seen through my own experience and that of many others, that we can nourish that deeper awareness until it becomes a true and vital understanding of our place in this world.

—Joseph Cornell,
Sharing Nature with Children

Schoolyard efforts in North America. In Canada the Evergreen Foundation began a nationwide project, School Ground
Naturalization in 1991. Nearly 400 schools have undertaken
creating natural outdoor classrooms, aided by the foundation's
newsletter and resource book *The Guide to School Ground
Naturalization: Welcoming Back the Wilderness.* One advantage
of naturalized school grounds, as articulated by the foundation, is greater environmental safety for children, because
herbicides or pesticides are not used, which are generally more
hazardous to children than to adults. Government, foundations,
and businesses cosponser the organization.[18]

The more locally focused Boston GreenSpace Alliance,
composed of numerous public, private, and foundation members, has begun a two-million-dollar, five-year program to
restore and revitalize 250 acres of schoolyards as public open
space for enhanced community life. Local community owner-
ship of planning and maintenance is a key feature.[19]

Habitats for wildlife. Several states have begun new efforts
to create wildlife habitats on school grounds. In Maryland, for
instance, workshops for teachers provide information on
planning habitats and obtaining funding for their development. Teachers learn about three kinds of habitats: wetlands,
meadows and butterfly-attracting gardens, and woods (refor-
estation projects). Planting a butterfly garden is relatively
easy; more complex is converting storm drain ponds into
wetlands, as several schools are doing. Maryland's project is a
collaboration between state government (education and natural resources), the federal government (Fish and Wildlife
Service), and the Chesapeake Bay Trust, a tax-supported
agency that aids Bay-related projects.[20] Habitat efforts are also
underway in New Hampshire, Virginia, Oklahoma, and Kan-
sas; Florida has an especially well-developed program.[21]

Gardens—a perennial in full bloom. Involving children
with gardens no doubt started with our distant agrarian ances-
tors and has continued unabated until recent times. The idea
of Paradise being a garden is an ancient one.[22] Contemporary
forms of children's involvement with growing things echo the
age-old affinity for gardens: children are gardening on vacant
lots in cities, inside classrooms in Alaska. Many garden
projects with school children are beautification—everyone
planting a bulb or a tiny pine tree; some are to produce food.
Others involve working with senior citizens or community
groups. Children benefit from gardens as they participate in

Places for Play

"...Nooks and hideaways where children fantasize and invent their own worlds"
—Roger Hart

Fantasy rides, group games, log climbing—all on an "ordinary" asphalt playground at the Coombes School in the outskirts of London

The Washington Environmental Yard (in Berkeley, California), a public school's expanse of asphalt transformed into ponds, woods, and meadows

© *Robin C. Moore*

© *Robin C. Moore*

© Ken Druse

The "Success Garden" in Harlem, a community oasis flourishing on once-vacant lots

© Ken Druse

A telescope fashioned from plentiful, fast-growing bamboo

At the Judith Resnik School in Gaithersburg, Maryland, protected courtyard ponds designed to be seen by children from a hall window

*F*loating platform with aquarium tanks for pond study at the River Farm in Alexandria, Virginia

the planning and design; experience the growth and life cycles, which are basic science understandings; develop habits of nurturance of life; and find satisfaction and pleasure in producing something beautiful and/or useful (sometimes a contrast with other forms of school work).

Arlene Martaurano, an elementary teacher in South Carolina who has gardened with children for 20 years, observes that gardening is also good for children who are new to using English (things grow no matter what language you speak). Requiring sustained, long-lasting efforts, gardening also promotes team building, as Martaurano points out, as well as providing exercise and nutrition, reducing the alienation between generations, and serving to integrate large amounts of curriculum.[23] Paris Ward, one of Martaurano's fifth-graders, adds that gardening can help children feel more positive:

> We enjoyed the garden very much. The kids who were always bad were very well behaved.[24]

Just as gardens are increasingly used as therapy for the ill,[25] they should be part of a healthy environment for the young.

Teachers often find gardens an appealing way to provide curriculum outdoors. Most teachers find it easy to bring in a shovel and let the children spade up a schoolyard corner for planting. Even easier, a teacher can simply plop down a bag of potting soil, cut holes to stick small plants in, and also cut holes in the bag's bottom for drainage. Helpful resources abound (see "Plants and Gardens" in Appendix A). Many local organizations, such as gardening clubs, offer help and stand ready for a good proposal from teachers.

With gardens attracting teachers and children both in and out of cities, urban gardeners, in particular, are likely to need to pay attention to soil quality. Much city soil holds lead and other toxic substances. Fresh soil should be brought in if testing reveals hazardous substances. If food is to be grown, more precautions are required.[26] Despite such difficulties, the process of growing food—a major task for the world now and in the future—gives children valuable information and experience in health and nutrition.

By giving children experiences in working on gardens, we affirm a constellation of values that are important to impart to children: demanding work; contact with the basics of weather, food, and soil; rewards roughly proportionate to the work put in; and a stewardship of the earth. Play proponents observe, however, that gardens do not hold all young children's interest, nor do they provide for a high level of individual creativity. On a

Requiring sustained efforts over weeks and months, gardening helps children learn and work together as a team.

cautionary note, maintaining gardens requires commitment and work that may end up falling to the adults. Or if a project involves the whole school, the older children can contribute substantially. If our goal is having our children appreciate nature, Roger Hart's observation gives guidance:

> Simply making greenhouses visually accessible on a daily basis for young children to see seedlings developing into beautiful plants (which can be managed by older children) might be just as valuable an opportunity as the chance to handle seedlings themselves.[27]

In *Gardening from the Heart*, Carol Olwell underscores Hart's point. Writing about summers on her grandparents' farm, a place lush with flowers and fields, she remembers playing in the creek with her sister and cousin.

> As I recall, we were never asked to help in the garden, and we probably didn't volunteer. So I didn't acquire any skills or knowledge about gardening from my grandmother. What I did absorb, as leaves absorb sunlight, was the sense that the earth was a truly beautiful and vibrant place, and that it deserved to be loved.[28]

Olwell's sense of appreciation became the basis for her adult interest in gardens and gardeners.

Helping children appreciate natural environments

Combining free play in a multichoice outdoor environment, with thoughtful teacher-led activities, can make being outdoors as valuable as being inside. There are numerous sources of ideas for activities listed in Appendix A (see "Outdoor Activities").

The teacher's role. Judith Dighe, an experienced teacher of young children in the outdoors, suggests that the teacher's most important role is sharing enthusiasm, curiosity, and wonder, as she quotes educator Joseph Cornell's dictum "Teach less, and share more."[29] She urges us to converse with children, avoiding quizzing and treating the outdoors as a list of names and qualities to be studied. Since young children are in the discovery stage in regards to the outdoors, Dighe believes,

> It's best to take cues from the children—listening, watching, sharing interest and delight first. Then ask questions that will help the child further her own investigation, answer questions to which you know the answer, and look up information together if the child wants to know.[30]

Being in natural environments and having a role model who validates one's interest in water, plants, and insects are key factors in becoming a person who cares about the environment.[31]

Magnifying glasses help children notice aspects of the natural world, as do "viewing tubes"(made from paper towel tubes) that focus the gaze. Dighe advises cautioning children not to disturb small ecosystems—overturned rocks and logs should be restored to their original position to protect the small creatures under them.[32]

To pick or not to pick. An unresolved issue for teachers is whether children should be allowed to pick wildflowers or other pieces of plants. The environmentalist ethic "Take only pictures, leave only footprints" is too abstract for young children who need to employ all their senses in exploring objects. Bess-Gene Holt advises teaching children in this way: "Pick what you plant. Leave wild growth alone, especially in natural settings."[33] While many of us agree that it is far preferable for children to pick, and pick apart, plants purposefully grown by us (which can include wildflowers), children should be allowed to pick dandelions and other plants that are clearly abundant survivors and should have access to nuts, berries, pinecones, leaves, and fallen objects. Such natural items were, after all, our species' first and only toys. Let's allow children this link to prehistory. Our current fashioning of

© Robin C. Moore

Fast-growing willows are an example of plants that children can freely pick without ruining the plant, and use as play props.

principles that allow us to live within and sustain our environment makes us face the inevitable contradictions involved. For example, we earnestly plant and nurture trees, yet know that Nature itself destroys thousands of trees in forest fires every year.

* * *

Teachers are in the front lines of developing new ethics for children and the environment. Taking the natural environment as a given is no longer possible. Other segments of the society also are helping reshape our relationship with the environment, as Chapter 6 discusses. But, next we turn to the subjects of playground safety and peace.

4

Safety Outdoors

Six-year-old Jason clambered to the top of the kindergarten playyard climber—an 8-foot tapered cylinder of metal bars—hung inside a few moments, lost his grip, and rattled down to the chip-strewn dirt below, cracking two ribs.

Jason typifies children hurt annually on American playgrounds. In 1992 approximately 170,000 children were injured on playgrounds severely enough to require emergency room treatment. About three-fourths of such injuries were caused by falls.[1] Every time a child is hurt on the school or center playground, teachers have to ask if the injury could have been prevented. Should the climber be replaced with a better one? Should we have a better surface under that climber? Shall we have a policy of "no mittens on the climber"? Shall we declare the climber off-limits on damp days? Does Jason need more supervision—is he pushing his limits these days?

Teachers also worry about parental response to accidents. Will we be charged with negligence? Will Jason be taken out of our school? Will other parents lose confidence? That children fall as a matter of course is one more area of parent education that today's teachers undertake. As Jambor and Palmer point out,

> Children are bound to fall, no matter how safe the playground equipment or surrounding area. Falling is a natural consequence of children's play actions and their practicing large-motor skills.[2]

Reducing playground injuries

Given that children will fall, what can be done to make these falls less injurious? Various studies and evaluations provide guidance for teachers, schools, and centers.

Surfaces. Many playgrounds still have concrete or asphalt surfaces even though common sense and many studies indicate that falling onto such hard surfaces hurts children more than falling onto sand or rubber or wood chips or pea gravel.[3] Getting rid of mud by covering heavily used surfaces with asphalt or concrete is one of those ideas that once seemed practical but clearly has become unacceptable. Frost summarizes the benefits and drawbacks of organic surfaces (e.g., bark, mulch, shredded wood) and inorganic loose materials (e.g., sand, pea gravel).[4] The *Handbook for Public Playground Safety* by the Consumer Product Safety Commission (CPSC) concludes that there are only two types of acceptable playground surfaces: "unitary materials"(usually rubber mats or rubberlike substances) or "loose-fill materials," such as mulch and pea gravel.

Critical Heights for Safety

| Tested materials | Uncompressed depth | | | Compressed depth |
	6-inch	9-inch	12-inch	9-inch
Wood mulch	7 ft.	10 ft.	11 ft.	10 ft.
Double-shredded bark mulch	6	10	11	7
Uniform wood chips	6	7	>12	6
Fine sand	5	5	9	5
Coarse sand	5	5	6	4
Fine gravel	6	7	10	6
Medium gravel	5	5	6	5

Note: Critical height is defined as "an approximation of the maximum height from which a life-threatening head injury would not be expected to occur." For further explanation see page 49.

Source: Consumer Product Safety Commission, *Handbook for Public Playground Safety* (Washington, DC: Government Printing Office, 1991), 21.

A summary review of the relative safety of commonly used loose-fill materials is shown in the box "Critical Heights." Critical height is the approximate maximum height from which a child could fall without a life-threatening head injury being likely to occur; 6 inches of loose wood mulch could protect a child falling about 7 feet; 12 inches would cushion an 11-foot fall.[5] Materials compacted through heavy use or weathering do not absorb a child's fall as effectively as freshly laid materials.

Other surface hazards, such as exposed roots, broken drains, or steps, can also cause falls to running children. Each play area needs to be inspected for such irregularities. Regular inspection is important because some hazards emerge over time; a severe rainstorm, for example, can erode the ground, exposing roots and rocks.

Equipment. The great metal structures of playgrounds from previous eras, the tall slides, the high climbers, the 20-foot swings, create unreasonable hazards for young children. Falls from these structures are long falls in which the child's speed increases, such that the resulting sudden stop on the ground is very forceful. Because these structures were so sturdily built, they have tended to last unless concerned adults have replaced them with lower, safer structures.

Some of these replacement structures have problems of their own. Creative, fanciful arrangements—aesthetically appealing to adults—don't always work for children's active play. Protuberances, decorations, and odd shapes not designed for actual interaction with bodies look interesting but catch coats, evade grips, and challenge children to invent ways of playing on them, which often turn out to be unsafe. What do you do with a large metal pumpkin anyway? The wooden creations preferred now by playground committees seem to have short lives, ending in splinters.

Frost categorizes hazards with equipment, including entrapment, heights, pinch and crush points, protrusions and sharp areas, suspended elements (cables, wires, ropes), slippery surfaces, railings. Nonequipment hazards include toxic materials, poisonous plants, and electrical items, such as switch boxes, air conditioners, and guy wires.[6]

Fortunately, increasing attention to playground safety has resulted in increased state and local regulation, some of which is documented in the recent publication of useful resources for teachers (described in Appendix B). The *Handbook for*

Public Playground Safety is a readable and well-researched document that is anticipated to serve as a standard of measure in litigation involving playground injury.[7]

The guides help underscore the fact that playground maintenance is as essential as building maintenance. Not only are playground surfaces and equipment susceptible to disrepair, but also their wider usage by the larger community often results in disregard of the need of children for a clean, safe area. Broken glass, trash, drug paraphernalia, and outright vandalism mar many school playgrounds and discourage teachers from using them with children. The cost of keeping playgrounds clean and in good repair is daunting. The cost of neglect, however, is probably many times higher over the long run.

More than buying and maintaining equipment

Frost observes that playground safety is a function of interrelated activities: design of the play area, design and installation of equipment, the maintenance, plus supervision by adults—combined with abilities and interests of child users.[8] Teachers want children to be safe, but safety should not preclude growth-producing challenges. A playground with nothing to climb on certainly keeps children from long-distance falls, but on a bare playground children tend to challenge one another, sometimes with injuries resulting. A prime cause of bullying on playgrounds is the lack of other things to do.[9]

Sufficient play activities encourage safe play. Kritchevsky and Prescott describe how to estimate how much there is to do on a playground. Count the number of spaces for a child—how many swings, how many wheel toys, how big a climber? If there are 8 spaces and 20 children, conflict is likely. Empty space is "potential"—it may or may not be used for play. The level of complexity is also important. Things that can only be used one way, such as a swing, do not engage children for as long a time as a sandbox with water and tools.[10] If a cursory count of play spaces reveals not enough to do, then the playground is not only not supportive of children's development and enjoyment, it is actually unsafe.

Safe, interesting play for young children generally requires that things be at hand to be moved, built with, rearranged. Fields and woods once naturally provided children with these objects; now adults must provide them: bringing blocks outside, setting

© Roger W. Neal

To be safe in natural environments, children need to learn about wild plants, insects, and animals.

In addition to improving school grounds, teachers and parents should plan opportunities for children to experience outdoor environments, such as streams, wetlands, beaver dams, working farms, and apiaries.

up dirt to dig, allowing sticks and ropes and pots and water. Playgrounds without "loose parts" are sterile and uncreative, and they impede children's social and intellectual development.

Preschool teachers, more often than not, recognize the importance of the outdoors for children's development. They provide sandboxes, ride-on toys, and climbing equipment, as well as easels brought outside, playdough, blocks, and other materials, and they provide the supervision and interaction needed to facilitate use of such items. It is a rare primary school, however, particularly in the public sector, that offers its children anything out-of-doors but large numbers of other children, a small amount of equipment including a few balls and jump ropes, and incredibly inadequate supervision and/or

Children do not "misuse" or "abuse" play equipment. They seek challenges and learning experiences in play, and this has a direct correlation to risk taking.

—Francis Wallach, *Parks and Recreation*

After I took my third-graders to the tidal pond in the neighborhood to study it, I noticed they were going there after school, too. So we talked about it a lot during class. They came up with most of the ideas on how to be safe there: always let your parents know where you are, always go with a buddy, know about the tides. I would ask them questions such as, "What would you do if someone fell in?" They would talk about the long-handled nets they used and staying away from the edge. I felt good about our discussions—we all learned that they could use the pond safely, yet enjoy and learn from it.

—Peggy Flohr, third-grade teacher

facilitation by adults. Typically, a recess-time aide watches over several classes of children, intervening only for egregious violations of safety or civility.

Changing an educational mentality in which children are simply "let out for recess" and nothing more, thus fostering aggressive unsafe play, is difficult when funds for education are shrinking and other conspicuous needs are emerging. Teachers will make the difference, asserting the essentialness of a safe and challenging outdoors for education and weaving outdoor experiences into their academic curriculum. Blatchford observes that formerly most classrooms were dull, rigid, and sterile, but now are bright with color and rich with resources; if we have evolved our thinking on classrooms, it is possible that we will come to regard school grounds with as much care.[11] A richly stocked outdoor environment is better and safer in every way.

Safety concerns in nature/wildlife habitat areas. An emerging trend toward establishing nature areas, including wildlife habitats, on school grounds raises new safety concerns for teachers. The main issues, according to environmentalist Lisa Schicker, involve poisonous plants, insects, and snakes, and hazardous site conditions. All hazard reduction involves educating children as an ongoing measure, but specific conditions require specific remedies as well. Steep banks and unstable slopes, particularly those ending in water, should be eased. Although eradicating all poison ivy on a large scale is impractical, in small, more immediate areas it should be done. Rock piles attract snakes, so they should be eliminated if there are poisonous snakes in the area.[12] Because U.S. geographic regions vary tremendously in their hazardous plants and animals, teachers, schools, and centers should inquire about their particular locale. The Cooperative Extension Service provides information and advice related to urban or rural settings.[13] Becoming familiar with and knowledgeable about possible hazards is the best way to guard against them, much better than avoiding the outdoors altogether.

Using the outdoors for field trips—safety concerns. Some teachers say that their neighborhoods are too dangerous to take the children walking through. Indeed, although the children may walk through such neighborhoods to and from school, as well as often reside in them, teachers are wise to be cautious. Teachers alone cannot ensure safety in a neighborhood, but the school in league with other neighborhood groups, particularly parents, can work toward this goal.

Many neighborhoods are peaceful and offer good opportunities for exploration. But each teacher should consider the school's neighborhood as extended classroom space and can find its distinctive elements to incorporate into her curriculum: a creek, statues or monuments, buildings of various materials,

---

Safety Precautions in Natural Environments

As you prepare to take your students into the schoolyard to conduct an inventory, consider the following safety precautions.

Different habitats require different clothing. If wandering in mowed, cleared areas, students should wear closed-toe shoes (preferably sneakers) and socks that are pulled up. Hats, caps, and shirts with sleeves will protect skin from the sun. If students are working in wooded areas or abandoned fields, they should wear long pants and socks (with socks pulled up over pant legs) and, in some seasons, insect repellent. Deer and dog ticks will occur in grassy areas; check exposed areas of the skin when returning from being outdoors.

Most schoolyard organisms can be examined and handled with no harm, or at most, scratches from thorns or bites from grasshoppers. Teach your students that careless handling can injure the plant or animal as well as the student.

Caution the students to avoid dense underbrush and not to reach into holes. Warn them not to eat any schoolyard plants and animals. Although most brightly colored fruits are harmless (some leave a bad taste in your mouth), others can be poisonous. Some mushrooms can be deadly poisonous; students should be warned never to eat a wild mushroom of any variety, even when a self-professed expert on wild mushrooms is present. As a precaution, students should wash their hands after handling mushrooms. In fact, it is a good idea for students to wash their hands immediately after any schoolyard activity.

vacant lots—all are there for the studying. Teachers should not retreat fearfully from the real world. As Francis Wardle says,

> We need to concentrate on visiting outdoor environments that allow children to explore, learn the marvels of nature, and experience some basic information about the world—in places such as parks, trails, wetlands, old quarries, streams, working farms, mountains, building sites, gardens, beaver dams, road construction sites, rock formations, etc.[14]

Assume that safe ways of visiting can be devised.

Children need us to teach them how to use out-of-classroom spaces. Teachers want to set expectations of learning and behavior and hold to them, modeling the idea that learning is everywhere, not just in the classroom. Traffic safety, a usual part of the primary curriculum, is important for field trips; in the same way, caution around wild plants and animals may, too, become part of the curriculum as schools broaden their scope. Some states have written materials to help teachers guide children in natural areas (see an example from New Hampshire's guide in the box "Safety Precautions").

The hairs on many local caterpillars irritate the skin or even give a sharp sting, as do the hairs on at least one common plant (stinging nettle). The damage potential of some organisms (bee, wasp, poison ivy) is well known, but do not assume that all of your students share in that knowledge. Poison ivy occurs frequently. A bee sting kit may be a wise addition to your school's first aid package. Teachers should already be aware of any children who have allergies to insect stings or certain pollens.

Contact with live or dead mammals should be avoided, as some carry disease that can infect humans. (Permits are required to collect certain wildlife specimens; check with your state wildlife agency.) Bites and scratches from wild mammals are potentially serious and should receive professional medical attention. For example, raccoons, who have adapted to life in human communities and do not usually fear humans, can carry diseases such as distemper and rabies.

A final caution. For the sake of plants and animals you investigate, please be ethical in your treatment of the wild creatures that share your school grounds. If you move animals to another site for observation, return them to the place of capture when you are done. Any logs, boards, or rocks that are turned over in the course of your investigations should be returned to their original positions.

Source: Reprinted by permission, from M. Wyzga, *Homes for Wildlife: A Planning Guide for Enhancement on School Grounds* (Concord: New Hampshire Fish and Game Department, n.d.), 58–59. (An adaptation from the Florida Game and Fresh Water Fish Commission *Handbook to Schoolyard Plants and Animals of North Central Florida* by P. Feinsinger and M. Minno. © Nongame Wildlife Program.)

* * *

Let us all hope that the growing concern over safety will be matched by a concern for giving children outdoor places filled with developmentally appropriate opportunities, in recognition of what has been taken from them by urbanization, cars and trucks, and social disorder. Children have to have the opportunity to take some chances, to stretch some of their limits. Risk taking is concomitant with growth. Their environments should not be hazardous, but neither should they be without challenge. And children will create challenge for themselves:

> Since the idea of play is to explore and maximize the potential of any play setting, children will test its use to the limits of their abilities . . . . Children will run up slides, jump out of swings and climb trees. Well-designed play settings reflect an understanding of children's behavior and provide for risk-taking without introducing hazards.[15]

Parents, teachers, and administrators need to construct a common understanding of what constitutes safe yet challenging play in their schoolyard. The next chapter discusses some ways teachers can help children play more peacefully with one another.

5

Peaceful Playgrounds

Red-faced and tense, second-graders Matt and Tevon shoved to the front of the line forming at the playground edge.

"He tripped me!" "He pushed first!"

Mrs. P, the playground aide, patted both sets of shoulders calmingly.

"OK, boys, cool it. We're going in."

Mrs. O, the second-grade teacher, observing just inside the doorway, sighed, "Another recess fight to unravel . . . . Think we'll get to science today?"

Although commonplace and familiar, recess fights are increasingly undesirable. Fights on the playground take up teaching time later in the classroom; they upset children and interfere with children's learning nonviolent means of handling conflict. Given the current level of social violence, particularly among young people, fights are worrisome omens of continuing disruption.[1] When children are in a situation in which they fear being attacked or get into frequent physical fights, they are less likely to be engaging in growth-producing, satisfying play. Teachers have every motivation to help children play peacefully. As previous chapters indicate, good outdoor space includes quiet areas for children to retreat to. Beyond providing good space, however, teachers can also help with social skills and motivation.

Early childhood teachers have been among the most dedicated proponents of teaching nonviolence. The task has fallen to them as socialization, but also, perhaps, because the sight of young children hurting one another is so painful that they have striven to find ways to help children resolve conflict nonviolently. "Use your words!" echoes in every preschool classroom. In addition to teachers' natural recoiling from violent behaviors among children, there are strong philosophical and practical reasons for teaching children to seek peace, which this chapter discusses. Ways and means of creating more peaceful playgrounds are also described.

Peace and conflict—the indissoluble connection

Conflict is a condition of human existence. So is peace. Philosopher and composer Herbert Brun advises us to think of peace as a need, like sleep and food. When we are hungry, we need food; we eat to meet the need, then start becoming hungry all over again. When we are tired, we sleep, meeting the need, and then awake to begin getting tired all over again. So it is with peace. When we are in conflict, we need peace; when we get it, then we can start to deal with our conflicts again.[2] Brun's idea— that peace is a basic need—is useful to teachers since we think of ourselves as being in the business of meeting needs.

We should teach children that peace is a need, not a byproduct of exhaustion or overpowering violence. As columnist and peace educator Colman McCarthy writes, we need to begin peace education in the primary grades.[3] Just as children must eat and sleep, they must create peace. McCarthy writes about the forces that create peace:

> Every problem we have, every conflict . . . will be addressed either through violent force or nonviolent force. No third option exists. . . . I believe in nonviolent force—the force of justice, the force of love, the force of sharing wealth, the force of ideas, the force of organized resistance to corrupt power. Fighting with those kinds of forces is the essence of nonviolence.[4]

When you consider that the toll of people killed in wars in this century is approaching 100 million and that children are killing children in communities across the United States, it becomes urgent that we mobilize our forces for peace.

© Chad J. Walker

In helping children to learn peaceful play skills, playground staff need to make it clear that violence is not tolerated on the playground.

Because playgrounds typically offer school-age children much more independence and less restraint than the classroom, it is particularly important when they are on the playground that they have the ability to resolve conflicts peacefully.[5] Peace education is not typically part of the elementary curriculum, although values/character education increasingly tends to be. In upper elementary and middle school, conflict resolution/mediation programs are taking hold, and there is a growing recognition of the importance of such programs in the early elementary grades. As Susanne Wichert points out in *Keeping the Peace*, a practical book of activities for nurturing peacemaking skills and feelings, teaching peace is an all-day, everyday proposition, involving relations between the adults, the climate and objectives of the school, the physical environment, adult–adult interactions, and adult–child interactions.[6]

Playground peace needs to be understood in the broader context of school peace. We have a tradition of letting children follow their impulses with minimal adult supervision at recess, but in many settings pervasive violence is a consequence of this practice. This custom of tolerating playground violence no longer serves us well. We are as a species evolving, as Csikszentmihalyi observes, and to the extent we can guide our evolution, let us try.[7]

Peaceful play skills can be learned

Children's ability to play well is important. Children whose skills enable them to interact positively with peers and adults get to play more. They make connection with their peers and are able to sustain communication. Many children do not have good skills, however, and playground interactions can create problems for them that are detrimental as well as disruptive, often carrying over to the classroom. Not surprisingly, current research suggests that children's peer interaction skills are highly linked with patterns of interactions with their parents: coercive parenting is highly correlated with children's aggres-

*H*appy hearts and happy faces,
Happy play in grassy places—
That was how, in ancient ages,
Children grew to kings and sages.

—Robert Louis Stevenson

Establishing peace is the work of education.

—Maria Montessori

sive behavior or withdrawness, and a reasoning, inductive style of parenting is highly correlated with cooperative, responsive behavior.[8] To the extent that interactional skills are teachable, rather than inherited, teachers have an important role.

Among the skills that children need to develop are observing one another and responding appropriately, being flexible and willing to accept others' ideas, offering ideas for play that appeal to other children, and taking turns. To a large extent, these skills are learned through play itself, simply because the play experience is so attractive to children that typically they do these things in order to keep it going; they are motivated to negotiate, take turns, and use the other skills of cooperation.

Primary-age children are particularly open to learning or honing interactional skills. Generally optimistic about themselves, generally trusting of adult leadership, eager to have good school lives, and able to think causally, primary children like to learn how to socialize. Using group games, teachers can help children experience good play and learn the skills that they can then use independently. Even the simplest games have an effect: in a primary school of 344 children, the before-school aggression was sharply reduced by establishing jump-rope and foot-race activities.[9]

Group games establish a friendly, cooperative climate

Teachers of young children have long encouraged children to participate in group games, such as Duck, Duck, Goose. Teachers also find, however, that as children grow into the primary grades many games that children used to learn from one another in neighborhood play are no longer known by children, and additionally that many games formerly favored now appear too competitive or too rough, for example, Crack the Whip and Kick the Can. The Opies' classic study, for instance, documented British children's games.[10] The recent publication of *New York City Street Games*,[11] with its explicit instructions and even the materials for classic urban pastimes, indicates change in what children in earlier periods knew and what children today know.

Tips for Safe Play

To promote safe, caring play throughout the year,

Use positive language. Positive language promotes positive behavior. A teacher's language should empower children and encourage them to practice positive behavior.

Focus on non-competitive, non-elimination games. Children have more fun and feel good when they actively participate in most or all of the game instead of being eliminated and watching others play. Non-competitive games help children focus on the fun part of games. Most children enjoy games more when not thinking about winning or losing.

Troubleshoot. Most games have potential trouble spots. For example, in Tag, some children may tag too aggressively. Anticipate trouble spots and plan ahead. Model and role play appropriate behavior before trouble begins.

Observe carefully. You can't anticipate every trouble spot, so once play begins, watch for problem situations. Take note of less troublesome incidents and role-play appropriate behavior later. For situations that demand immediate attention, stop play and encourage the group to help solve the problem. For example, you might ask, "What do you think is the best thing to do in a situation like this?" (Expect a lot of stop points during the first few weeks of school.)

Time out for small infractions. Once rules have been established and success-fully practiced, establish "time out" for minor infractions. This helps check inappropriate behavior before a situation gets out of control.

Source: Reprinted by permission of Northeast Foundation for Children, from M.K. Clayton, "Peace on the Playground: Teaching Care, Friendliness, and Cooperation," *A Newsletter for Teachers* 4 (fall 1992): 5.

In view of such change, teachers now may need to help children learn games,[12] filling in for what older siblings, neighborhood children, and parents used to do. Teachers, too, do not need to be bound by tradition in choosing games;[13] they can choose the ones that provide the most fun and greatest satisfaction to children.

Fortunately, several excellent resources for games exist, some of which are listed in Appendix A (see "Playground Games"). Teachers working together to play some of these games find it easier to teach them to children. At the Northeast Foundation for Children/Greenfield Center School in Massachusetts, for example, over several years teachers have collaboratively worked out strategies to help all children participate in cooperative playground games. The basic strategies, which reflect a group-process approach, are fully elaborated in the foundation's news-letter and are summarized as follows:

1. Introduce the game playing to children in a group discussion.

2. Discuss, model, and role-play commands that are useful for all games, such as "freeze" and "circle up," and rules, such as walking and running safely, including everyone on teams, and helping one another.

3. Practice the game before actually playing it.

4. Add new games to the repertoire often to keep children's interest high.

5. Discuss the game inside after playing, allowing children to bring up both positive and negative experiences and feelings they had while playing.[14]

If a whole school undertakes such strategies, after a month or so of learning games and general rules, children from various classes can form their own games at recess. Making sure that all children learn all new games throughout the year and that staff members monitor the playing helps to ensure that all participants enjoy the play (see also the box "Tips for Safe Play").

Using group process to curb bullying

Group-process strategies similar to those outlined above have also been used in a wide-scale campaign in Norway to restrict bullying on school playgrounds.[15] Although the children were upper-elementary and secondary level in the Norway study, the principles were successfully applied. Schools determined that having peaceful playgrounds was a desirable school goal. Teachers were involved in playground activity, planning for it in class and supervising it. Teachers and staff set expectations and helped children develop workable rules. Teachers used class time to process with children their playground experiences and help them to develop better relations through cooperative learning activities. The entire population of each school entered into the effort to end bullying. Because bullying diminished sharply in the Norway campaign schools, the conclusion was that school people know how to end bullying. What is needed is a "willingness to involve ourselves" in making playgrounds safer.[16]

Other ways of creating conditions for peace

In addition to involving the whole school in working toward peaceful play behaviors, there are several other factors teachers and principals can consider.

Schools need to actively nurture children's peacemaking skills and attitudes, both in outdoor play and in the classroom.

1. Are the children separated by age? Younger children are often intimidated or overrun by older ones. Delineated play areas and separate recess times ease this. Multi-age groups have advantages if properly supervised.[17]

2. Are there enough adults (aides, trained parents, teachers) to provide interactive supervision? To ensure that schoolwide expectations of peaceful behavior are met, adults must be there encouraging the positive and discouraging the negative.

3. Are procedures for entering and exiting the play area sensible? All children lining up at the same time to enter the building causes dead time and boredom, with the usual consequences. All entering the building at the same time creates noise and crowding. Every school has its own physical configuration, but teachers and principals can devise ways to let children enter and exit with less large-group regimentation and thereby reduce conflict and confusion. Similarly, eliminating bells and buzzers

All over the schoolyard, we have plenty of niches for a child to take refuge in—from a friend or an aggressor. Or for quiet play.

—Susan Humphries, Coombes School

creates a more respectful atmosphere that contributes to peaceable behavior during transitions to and from the classroom.

4. Can recess or outdoor time be scheduled more flexibly, with individual classrooms fitting it into the flow of their other activities? Less arbitrary scheduling generally is more conducive to relaxed behavior. On the other hand, flexible scheduling creates logistical challenges. Also, the predictability of a break at a certain time can be reassuring to both children and teachers. Blatchford surveyed several schools on this issue and found mixed reactions to the idea of flexible scheduling.[18] Perhaps each school could consider such scheduling in the individual school's context.

5. Does the playground offer opportunities for children to care for the environment? Are there plants, animals, recyling bins? Does the playground give the appearance of being cared for by the adults? Children who learn to live harmoniously and caringly with the environment are learning "an essential part of living in harmony with other people."[19]

The whole school should work on peace

Peaceful outdoor behavior is related to peaceful indoor behavior. Schools that encourage children to participate in and take responsibility for governance and curriculum help children both to control their aggression and to value their own peaceful actions. Additionally, schools in which teachers help children challenge stereotypes, including those of race, gender, physical abilities, and culture, lessen the pressure on children and create spaces where new, more equitable relations may be explored. Reflecting on the lessons from her studies of gender relations in schools, Barrie Thorne advises,

> As adults, we can help kids, as well as ourselves, imagine and realize different futures, alter institutions, craft new life stories. A more complex understanding of the dynamics of gender, of tensions and contradictions, and of the hopeful moments that lie within present arrangements, can help broaden our sense of the possible.[20]

When children learn to live harmoniously and caringly with the environment, they are learning an important part of living in harmony with other people.

A belief in the possible—imagine a playground without fights (a world without wars!)—can lead to action.

Action is usually complex. We need to teach children how to nurture and display their peace-generating behaviors as well as to support them with environments designed to help them play well. Providing these good environments is not the concern solely of the schools. In fact, in the broader community, numerous efforts occur, which the next chapter discusses.

6

Broader Community Efforts

Today stressed systems of maintenance and security
have called into question the idea of public space as
a public good. The democratic concept of open,
friendly congestion is being undermined as parks,
playgrounds, and plazas become havens of crime
and drug-dealing. Public spaces, created to serve
noble purposes, are being put to ill use. . . . [We]
require public spaces. . . . We need our moments of
tranquility and inner peace, our reminders of the
rhythm of the planet. . . . places to exercise our
bodies and our spirits, as well as opportunities for
social congregation and friendly encounter.

—*New York City Parks Council*
and Central Park Conservancy

Fortunately, from the viewpoint of providing children good
places to play outdoors, we are experiencing a renewal of national consciousness of the environment and how to restore and
sustain it globally. Although this renewal is not directed at children, its success can benefit them in terms of a cleaner world and
more respectful attitude toward living things.

Young children will not immediately benefit from efforts to
save endangered species and national forests; these efforts are too
remote from their daily existence. Children will benefit immediately from improved schoolyards and neighborhoods. Considering the concept of endangered species, however, we can regard

children as one of them, in light of their vanishing habitats for play as well as the various kinds of pollution that complicate their lives and the lives of adults.

Thinking of children as endangered shapes what we do for them. School people—teachers, administrators, and others—admittedly have limited powers to change neighborhoods but are potent when they work in conjunction with others in the community. This chapter presents good efforts to improve children's habitats, with the thought that knowledge of allies empowers us.

Worldwide interest in play

Environmental psychologist Sanford Gaster, surveying the history of children in American cities, observes that while earlier eras gave sporadic but selfless attention to children's outdoor needs by establishing parks and programs, more recently children have been ignored. He concludes,

> Urban planning and policy that is conscious of children's needs has been absent from the national scene for the past 60 years. More than that, it is something that has moved farther from the public mind each era.[1]

Bringing children back into the public consciousness in regards to the importance of providing play opportunities is exemplified by two relatively recent scholarly publications: *International Play Journal* (in 1993) and *Children's Environments* (since 1984). A related resource, although not as focused, is Educational Resources Information (ERIC) for Science, Math, and Environmental Education in Columbus, Ohio, which is accessible through many public and university libraries.

International Association for the Child's Right to Play (IPA).
A human rights organization founded in Denmark in 1961 and composed of persons from many professions and countries, IPA holds play to be as much a right as shelter, food, health, and education. "The Declaration of the Child's Right to Play" (see Appendix D for a more complete description of IPA) identifies negative influences on children's development and proposes actions to ameliorate them. IPA's broad scope encompasses outdoor play.

Efforts to provide play spaces

Across the country, private organizations, governmental bodies, and occasionally land developers, sometimes in collaboration, provide useful models for restoring safe play places to children.

More than one thousand "greenways" now exist in the United States.

Greenways. Greenways are what The Conservation Fund calls "corridors of protected open space managed for conservation and recreation purposes."[2] Both public and private, they link waterways, nature reserves, parks, cultural features, and historic sites with one another and with places where people live. An extensive system of greenways would form a network of trails accessible to everyone within a 15-minute drive of home or work. While the idea of accessible trails is not new (the Appalachian Trail, for example, was established in 1921), it has received fresh impetus in the last few years, as noted by two U.S. Government reports on the outdoors and trails.[3] In 1991 Congress passed the Intermodal Surface Transportation Efficiency Act (ISTEA), specifying the construction of bicycle and foot trails as part of the nation's transportation infrastructure and providing some funding for the construction.[4] State departments of transportation administer the funding through local transportation agencies.

More than being paths and trails, however, greenways also are potential classrooms for children. Anne Lusk, chair of the Vermont Trails and Greenways Council, urges teachers and others to get involved in building greenways—at least 108,000—one for every school in the nation.[5] To date, there

*Community Efforts—***69**

We need safe parks and healthy recreation activities to keep our kids off the streets and out of gangs.

—Los Angeles Police Chief Willie Williams

are more than 1,000, with approximately 600 of them being old railroad beds. States having very active greenways projects include Washington, Oregon, California, Ohio, Vermont, Pennsylvania, Maryland, and West Virginia. The cities of Houston and Denver have distinctive urban trails.[6]

Similar in focus to greenways are suburban and rural yards and fields in which the use of perceptive native management encourages flora and fauna. Since 1973, the National Wildlife Federation's Backyard Habitat Program has assisted citizens and communities in such management.[7] In her book *Noah's Garden*, Sara Stein writes about linking our yards and fields, these private spaces, that they may become "public spaces" for plants and animals. She envisions "a continuity of living quarters" across the country that would allow plants and animals to freely disperse as is their wont.[8] Having rejuvenated her own six acres, Stein comments on the near demise of the wild turkey:

> Perhaps wild turkeys can return; perhaps they can't. But when each of us, alone and in community, on acreage and in small back yards, for reasons of ecology, economy, or style has done all that can be done to restore the abundance of the land, many other animals will surely rejoin us.[9]

Stein's vision empowers us.

Urban initiatives. Cities all over the world are coping with the pressures of cars, people, pollution, and poverty.[10] Here in the United States, exemplary efforts are underway in some cities. In Baltimore the Urban Forestry Program of the U.S. Department of Agriculture (USDA) Forest Service[11] administers a $500,000 grant for an interagency collaborative model program to restore the environment (watersheds and streams, reforestation, community gardens), with community initiatives, youth jobs training (for example, the new National Civilian Community Corps), and leadership development. The program, "Revitalizing Baltimore," unites the efforts of federal, state, and city governments, plus private institutions (Yale University, Outward Bound, and environmental organizations). The project's goals include promoting community activities to make Baltimore a better place to live, work, and play; encouraging and supporting stewardship of natural resources; and giving community volunteers, youth, and city staff the skills to conduct their own environmental restoration projects.[12] What's encouraging about this project is that it focuses on the link between a physically degraded environment and a poor quality of life for young people, offering resources for interactively improving both.

In New York City where public spaces were once a source of pride and civic health but, as a result of the post-World War II distractions and upheavals, have become shabby, inadequate, and dangerous, the Parks Council and Central Park Conservancy have developed a thoughtful and farsighted master plan, *Public Space for Public Life: A Plan for the Twenty-first Century*.[13] Acknowledging the many grassroots efforts underway in the city, the document lays out areas of concern: neighborhood parks top the list, followed by urban wilderness, greenways, waterfronts, streets, and sidewalks. Identifying 100 "priority neighborhoods" where dense populations, high

© Steffi Graham

Sharp, sticky, and fragrant pine needles—children growing up in cities too often miss out on such experiences, but urban projects like "Revitalizing Baltimore" show that many wonders can flourish in the heart of the city.

poverty, and crime are accompanied by few and ramshackle parks, the report calls for

> The creation of a cluster of parks within walking distance of each priority neighborhood on vacant city-owned land. The cluster would include a "central park" of about two acres and four smaller "satellite" parks, or green open spaces.
>
> Two acres of vacant land can do for an urban neighborhood what Manhattan's Central Park does for the entire city—provide an outdoor living room for family and community life. With gardens, picnic areas, playgrounds, playing fields, and enclosed recreation centers, a community central park can accommodate many different activities and put them all within reach of an entire neighborhood. Smaller lots can function as satellite extensions of central parks, providing small playgrounds, garden plots, and sitting areas for young children, parents, and the elderly. These green, open spaces would constitute a community mini-park system. They would be not only a welcome change from rubble-filled vacant lots, but a tangible sign of community commitment and renewal.[14]

For an example of such a park (pictured in "Places for Play" following page 42), see the box "School and Community Collaboration." The report asks for $195 million dollars for setting up new neighborhood parks and $20 million per year for staffing them.[15] As discussed in the next section, staffing the parks is deemed essential to provide education, safety, and maintenance. The report concludes, recalling the original inspiring vision of public spaces:

> Democratic meeting grounds, places of amiable and useful congregation, where under the most beneficial circumstances people from different backgrounds could learn how much they had in common. The parks and public spaces fostered prosperity and instilled democratic values.[16]

This well-stated, generous vision of the potential of parks regrettably, as of this writing, lacks funding.[17] Nonetheless, we should foster it in the interest of our young children.

Staffed parks—better play possible. More trained adults in public play spaces would allow a broader range of play opportunities for children. Several countries in Northern Europe train persons directly for that purpose, not as park rangers, but as play facilitators. Adventure playgrounds require child-centered staff. In Huntington Beach, California, such a playground is part of the city park system; its pond is replete with rafts and a rope bridge; its fort–building site, mudslide, and 50-foot cable swing are overseen by a staff of six. Unusual in American park systems, this playground has existed 20 years; nearby cities of Lorba Linda and Irvine have similar publicly run playgrounds, as does Berkeley, California.

School and Community Collaboration Makes an Urban Oasis

[Organizing community institutions to develop gardens] began in 1989, under the auspices of Public School 175 in Central Harlem. Working with seven grade-school kids, landscape architect Karneal Thomas came up with plans for a vacant lot across from the school. Students and volunteers helped clear, fence and plant it.

• Today, from the street, the Success Garden looks like a solid community garden.

• It's open to the public and during the week there's often a science class in session and kids playing.

• The row of vegetables looks healthy; there's a small playground with a rubberized surface and a gazebo. But it's not until you get inside the garden that you can appreciate the extent of what has been accomplished.

• The green space snakes back behind a couple of 100-year-old tenements, opening up into a lot where there's another vegetable garden and a small pond that will be stocked with fish.

• Beyond that, it connects to yet another lot, this one recently cleared by a local development corporation and awaiting planting.

• An empty lot down at the other end of the block may eventually be hooked up into the garden as well.

It is an almost utopian vision, a garden-city block in the middle of Central Harlem. You could hardly plan it better if you started from scratch.

Source: Reprinted by permission, from H. Lindgren, "Grassroots Security," *Landscape Architecture* 85 (February 1995): 54. © 1995 *Landscape Architecture Magazine.*

The recreation department in Montgomery County, Maryland, near Washington, D.C., has developed even another role for playground staff: formalized conflict mediation education. Teenage volunteers in the Recreation Resolution Corps spend a minimum of four hours per day, five days a week, teaching small groups of children conflict-resolution skills—how to state the problem, to identify feelings about the problem, and to suggest mutually agreeable solutions. These same skills are taught in the county schools, thus providing the children consistency in learning. School staff provide the training for the volunteers, who are considered an integral part of the summer recreation program.

School–park partnerships. While the Recreation Resolution Corps is a contemporary example of cooperation between school boards and park departments, it is neither a new concept nor one widely practiced. The Fountain School in Grand Rapids, Michigan, described in Chapter 2, exemplifies school and park collaboration, with the schoolyard integral to the parkland. Another illustration is the "Lighted Schoolhouse Program" in Milwaukee, which for 75 years has allowed schools to be used on evenings, weekends, and in the summer, thanks to a common effort by the city government and school board—a practice that is being adopted in many communities around the United States. The President's Commission Report observed in 1987 that fiscal restraints "have made it difficult for communities to adopt these programs [but] the costs of such cooperation are small in comparison to the substantial benefits of using school facilities for public recreation."[18]

"Child-aware" land development. Planned communities, such as Columbia, Maryland, and Reston, Virginia, have sought to provide for children's need to get around their neighborhoods without being endangered by cars. Tunnels under roads and pedestrian/bike paths are standard in such communities. Futurists such as Robert Thayer envision neighborhoods where cars rather than children are constrained (see the box "How Neighborhoods Could Be"). Village Homes, a California development that is the inspiration of Thayer's vision, provides children with open drainage channels and ponds (which work to prevent rapid storm runoff), greenways, central turf areas, vineyards, orchards, community gardens, a playground, and a swimming pool.[19] An observational study of children's use of the neighborhood during a week late in spring reveals that 65% of the activity occurred in green open spaces, 24% along bike paths in common areas and along drainage swales. Streets were the second most popular site (20%).[20] Very little play occurred in private open spaces, such as patios and backyards. Children were also asked what were their favorite places:

> The most sacred places for children were wild or unfinished places such as building areas and places with names like "willow pond" and "clover patch." These findings argue for neighborhood design that retains open space in its natural state, which children can manipulate to suit their own needs.[21]

Adult tastes determine what builders provide—adults who demand some child-accessible, unfinished, "wild" places will get them for their neighborhood's children. Using design criteria to develop such places can help rehabilitate residential areas devoid of natural habitats (see the box "Design Criteria").

In most cities, vacant lots serve as wild areas. Vacant lots have an ambiguous reputation, but the main thing they are vacant of is houses or other buildings. If a school organizes community forces to reclaim and maintain a vacant lot for children's play, all that teachers might consider removing are only the dangerous items (things that can cut, puncture, or otherwise harm children). Daily

How Neighborhoods Could Be

I gaze at the older neighborhoods and realize how much they have changed. Protection of farmland has turned most urban development inward. Density has increased greatly, with much more in-fill development . . . . The formerly wide streets are now leaner and greener, much of the pavement having been reclaimed for bicycle and shuttle lanes, torn up for shade tree planting strips, or designated for community open space. The bare-asphalt street glare which burned our eyes on summer days years ago is nearly gone as a result of the pressures to densify older neighborhoods, yet make them cooler and more livable.

Hardly any newer home has a large front yard anymore; many townhouse developments feature the Play-Park concept, where cars access housing clusters by way of landscaped community plazas. As "guests" in this pedestrian and recreation-dominated environment, vehicles share the courtyards with kids playing basketball and all the other [activities] . . . . Everyone likes this concept; the plazas are designed for people first; kids can play safely, and old folks can walk down the middle of the street without risking being run over and killed. Car speed limits are 5 m.p.h. . . . Not as much parking is needed these days either, since most families only own one vehicle . . . .

I guess what was most difficult to finally get through the heads of city officials and developers was the need for all neighborhoods to be connected in some fashion to an open space and wildlife habitat corridor. . . . When the new pedestrian-style urban development really took hold in the late 1990s, it took nearly 10 years for. . . developers to realize how much more critical "nearby nature" had become as a payoff for all that extra density. Finally they came around. . . . We may be starting to get it right.

—Robert L. Thayer, Jr.

cleanup of such items is vital, just as it is indoors. The value of vacant lots is not only in the loose parts provided but also in their ecological triumph of adaptation and survival, "as much a feat of nature as a flowered New England roadside or any shaded prairie grove."[22] Not a bad model for urban children to contemplate!

"Calming traffic"—an idea we ought to embrace

Vehicles pose one of the most overpowering threats to children's outdoor play. We have to seriously consider altering our use of and attitudes toward them.

Our ambivalence about cars. On a five-lane street near my suburban house, the speed limit was raised from 35 to 45 miles per hour a couple of years ago to handle more cars. By now three pedestrians have been killed. This particular street has long been a boundary for the neighborhood children, who understood—"No way can you cross that street, not until you're twelve."

On another boundary street, citizens got the county transportation department to reduce the speed limit and reshape the straight-

Design Criteria for Wildlife Places

Landscape design criteria for children (ages 6 to 10) and wildlife

Criteria	Most preferred	Acceptable (rank order)
Habitat types	Aquatic; preferably stream with vegetated corridor.	Other aquatic areas; wetlands, ponds, lakes. Forest, vacant lot, grassy field.
Location	Five-minute walk from home; central to neighborhood, linked to other wildlands.	Five-minute bicycle ride from home; along bike paths, sportsfields.
Size	Not important to kids, preferably 2 acres for wildlife.	
Shape	Greenbelt with activity nodes.	Large, circular shape.
Safety	Social safety.	Physical safety.

Plant and animal considerations in landscape design for children

Consideration	Most important	Less important
Animals to encourage	Salamanders, toads, frogs, turtles, insects, crayfish, squirrels, lizards, butterflies.	Songbirds, chipmunks, raccoons, non-poisonous snakes, opossums, birds of prey.
Animals to discourage	Poisonous snakes, stinging insects.	
Plants to encourage	Berry and fruit trees and shrubs edible to both children and wildlife. Good climbing trees.	Combination of native plants: evergreen and deciduous, all different height layers.
Plants to discourage	Poisonous or irritants: poison ivy and nettles.	Thick and impenetrable thorny brambles.

Source: Reprinted by permission, from L. Schicker, "Design Criteria for Children and Wildlife in Residential Development," *Integrating Man and Nature in the Metropolitan Environment*, eds. L.W. Adams and D.L. Leedy (Columbia, MD: National Institute for Urban Wildlife, 1987), 101.

away with protuberances that narrowed the roadway every so many yards. Neighborhood reaction was negative—"How come they get all that special treatment?" and "That stuff doesn't slow me down at all, I slalom it!"

On a third boundary street, which traffic had made a raceway, citizens posted signs, marched in protest of the danger, and planted bushes to narrow the road's shoulders. As circumstances happen, the road was a state highway, and the state undertook its major renovation, making the street a single lane for a year. Anyone who has taken on traffic problems will recognize all of the familiar actors here—layers of governments and citizens taking several and sometimes conflicting roles (commuters, parents, property owners). The three scenarios also show how ambivalent we are about cars—we want to use them, but we don't want to be endangered or bothered by others' use of or restrictions on them.

Ways of calming traffic. Cities all over the world face similar problems. Many European cities have altered their roads to calm traffic, which involves, as described above, adding trees, bushes, flower beds, play areas, and narrowings, as well as reduced speeds—"gentle inducements that make drivers proceed slowly and yield the right-of-way to pedestrians, cyclists, and children at play."[23] Rush-hour restrictions is another means. In judging if a street is safe for play, Robin Moore offers, "at somewhere between five and ten cars per hour... [the street] as a playspace becomes untenable—depending very much on the average speed of the vehicle and who the drivers are" (neighborhood residents pay more attention).[24] Germany and the Netherlands extensively employ traffic-calming strategies on both main and residential streets, and other northern European countries, Australia, and Japan are also trying these methods.

An intense form of calming is creating *woonerven*, a Dutch practice of redesigning or creating sections of residential streets to encourage children's play and outdoor activity and to discourage traffic (see illustrations on page 78). *Woonerven* have legal status in Germany and the Netherlands. Curbs are taken out; children are allowed to play in the whole street; cars must move at walking speed; parking spaces are clumped and located out of the way of children and other street users. Plantings, benches, and other additions signal livability. Barriers and signs alert motorists of a *woonerf*. A before-and-after study of two streets that became *woonerven* in Germany showed that children's play expanded into the newly available space and children played outside more, interacted more with one another and with objects they found in the street or brought with them, rode wheel-toys more, and engaged in more fantasy play, music making, and dancing.[25]

Traffic can also be calmed by increasing mass transit, reducing the number of parking places in downtown areas, and having motorists bear the true, full cost of operating a car (e.g., reduce government subsidies of oil companies that keep gas prices low). These strategies may be unpalatable to many people, including teachers, who use their cars heavily in transporting materials and yet receive such modest salaries that they would keenly feel the

To create a **woonerf,** *or residential street, from a street with ordinary automobile access, European planners take out curbs and add features, such as plantings, bollards, and benches. The* **woonerf** *sign alerts motorists.*

© Gustave Carlson

pinch of higher gas prices. Nonetheless, to restore neighborhood play to young children, we are going to have to restrain cars, as other countries have demonstrated is possible.

Be aware, be active. "All politics is local," said the longtime Speaker of the House Tip O'Neill, and so are all neighborhoods. To create or to preserve places for children to play outdoors, teachers need to look at what is around, then support the good ideas and fight the bad. Organizations and initiatives described in this chapter share our goals, if not fully, at least in part, and can help in realizing them.

Restoring the Birthright

We are of the soil and the soil is of us. We love the
birds and beasts that grew with us on this soil. They
drank the same water as we did and breathed the same
air. We are all one in nature. Believing so, there was in
our hearts a great peace and a willing kindness for all
living, growing things.

—*Luther Standing Bear*

Humans are amazingly adaptive and seem able to live in
very diverse environments. However, all of this diversity has
historically involved much more contact with the outdoors, in
particular the unbuilt part, than children now experience in
the United States.

Children, especially, have had access to the outdoors. In the
past, our houses were small, streets or fields were available,
automobiles didn't exist to imprison or threaten, and hardly
anyone went much to school. Knowing the newness of
children's being isolated from the outdoors, shouldn't we pay
more attention to this deficit? And with everything we know
about children's learning through their senses, shouldn't we be
determined to provide them with more than books and
screens that offer information only to ears and eyes—not a
fragrance or pungence, nor a softness or wetness, nor an

unexpected slither across a path just where one's foot was about to land?

Remember the king who wanted to see if Hebrew was the first language spoken, so he isolated a baby in a room to see what language emerged? Of course, no language emerged. Isolating children from the outdoors where so much happens, where there is so much to learn, might mean that no full human beings emerge.

Particularly when we consider "neighborhood children,"[1] this isolation appears adverse. Developmentally, they should be gaining the ability to navigate their immediate environs (in safety) and to construct for themselves the geography of their daily lives, thereby laying the foundation for the courage that will enable them eventually to lead their own lives.

Naturally, it is foolish to idealize children's lives in earlier times. Examples of children being exploited for their competence as street vendors, toddler tenders, textile and rug weavers are evident throughout the developing nations, reminding us that our own child labor laws were not passed until well into this century. In addition, the comprehensive public schooling that we, like other developed nations, have creates more opportunities for personal development than earlier and elsewhere. Still, those children who are less restricted in their access to the outdoors will surely gain competence in moving through the larger world.

It is particularly worrisome that children are being disconnected from what we call "nature." We ourselves are part of nature, having evolved along with the other plants and animals. We ought to take more heed of our habitats, knowing their loss is a primary cause for species extinction. The biophilia hypothesis presented in the first chapter seems more likely true than not. Most of us do respond, at least with interest and respect, to living things, plants or animals.

Since so many factors in contemporary life combine to restrict children from the natural world, it is incumbent on school people and others who work with children to help them reconnect with the natural world—the sky, the wind, the rain, the trees and plants, the streams and ponds. The grounds of schools and child care centers are particularly important places for this reconnection to begin because children spend so much time there, and the two institutions focus on children's welfare. A study of British schoolchildren indicates that children are keenly aware of their schoolyards, preferring the natural to the built aspects and liking places having "millions of bits" to play with and ones in which to hide, to climb, to explore, and to sit; the children also were highly critical of the adults who neglected the playground, allowing trash and broken equipment.[2] These children seemed to yearn to be immersed in natural artifacts and to feel disappointed without them.

* * *

To create school and center grounds that help replace the lost access to natural environments is a pressing task. Fortunately, we are coming to realize that "back-to-basics" short-changes children intellectually, but a rich and integrated curriculum, the kind that needs the reality of the outdoors, serves children well. When we serve children well, we predicate a better future.

Education is better when it is not limited to classrooms and better when play undergirds it. Fortunately, too, at this point in history, we find our allies are in the environmental movement and among those who care about children's play opportunities being throughout every environment. Teachers of young children, with their historical commitment to caring for the whole child, should be among those who lead the way to better play places everywhere that children are—schools, child care centers, streets, parks, greenways—and in leftover areas where children might explore and create their own places of interest and delight.

Notes

Preface, page iv

1. B.B. Whiting & C.P. Edwards, *Children of Different Worlds* (Cambridge, MA: Harvard University Press, 1988).

Chapter 1, pages 1–15

1. E.F. Provenzo, Jr., notes the sexism, racism, xenophobia, and violence of video games in *Video Kids: Making Sense of Nintendo* (Cambridge, MA: Harvard University Press, 1991). Lessons from video games are probably antithetical to attitudes of appreciation for the outdoors.
2. R. Louv devotes a chapter to this topic, "The Nature of Childhood," in *Childhood's Future* (Boston: Houghton Mifflin, 1990).
3. B. Berenson, *Sketch for a Self-Portrait* (Toronto: Pantheon, 1949), 18.
4. E. Cobb, *The Ecology of Imagination in Childhood* (New York: Columbia University Press, 1977), 33.
5. See A. Dargan & S. Zeitlin, *City Play* (New Brunswick, NJ: Rutgers University Press, 1990), for a rich description of play in New York City over the last 150 years.
6. R.C. Moore, "Streets as Playgrounds," in *Public Streets for Public Use*, ed. A.V. Moudon (New York: Columbia University Press, 1991), 45–62.
7. Dargan & Zeitlin, *City Play*, 152.
8. Dargan & Zeitlin, *City Play*, 155.
9. M. Hillman & J.G.U. Adams, "Children's Freedom and Safety," *Children's Environments* 9, no. 2 (1992): 10–21.
10. Commenting on the overall level of danger for children, M.W. Edelman states, "At least 13 children die daily from guns, and at least 30 other children are injured every day," in "Cease Fire! Stopping the War Against Children," *Harvard Medical Alumni Bulletin* (autumn 1994): 21. K.K. Christoffel reviews related statistics and analyzes the current thinking on how to end the gun death epidemic (now about 10 times larger than the polio epidemic at its height) in "Handguns and the Environments of Children," *Children's Environments* 12, no. 1 (1955): 39–48.

    One response to this uncontrolled violence against children has been entrepreneurial: at least two national businesses have built indoor playgrounds and charge a fee for children to play. There are climbers, slides, and bins of balls. Sodas, pizzas, popcorn, and candy are prominently featured.
11. United Church of Christ Commission for Racial Justice, *Toxic Wastes and Race in the United States: A National Report on the Racial and Socio-Economic Characteristics of Communities with Hazardous Waste Sites* (New York: Commission for Racial Justice, 1987), xiv.

    Furthermore, as farmland is increasingly built over, attention must be paid to pesticide and herbicide residues. In New Paltz, New York, land around an office building was found to have 186 times the lead level of ordinary soil and 48 times the arsenic levels, due to its prior use as an apple orchard that was sprayed with lead arsenate. See J. Steinberg, "Environment Agency Has Pollution Problem," *New York Times*, 6 March 1995, B6, Northeast edition.
12. Environmental Protection Agency, "Experimental UV Index," press release EPA 430-F-94-021, June 1994.
13. Australian children routinely wear hats and sunscreen because of the high incidence of skin cancer in Australia. The ozone hole over the Antartica causes routine use of sunblock and dark glasses by inhabitants of Punta Arenas, the world's southernmost city, at the tip of South America. See C. Sims, "A Hole in the Heavens (Chicken Little Below?)," *New York Times*, 8 March 1995, A4, Northeast edition.
14. The days of nearly all mothers being home, in crime-free neighborhoods, and sharing a "broad unspoken consensus" about acceptable behavior, probably will not come again, but D.B. Fink argues that school-age child care most closely replicates the advantages of those neighborhood experiences. See his "School-Age Child Care: Where the Spirit of Neighborhood Lives," *Children's Environments Quarterly* 3, (summer 1986): 9–11.
15. A study in Great Britain reveals that in 1971 while 89% of 9-year-olds got themselves to school (walking or biking), by 1990 less than 30% did. Comparable figures for 7- and 8-year-olds were 80% (1971) and 9% (1990). See M. Hillman, J. Adams, & J. Whitelegg, *One False Move . . . : A Study of Children's Independent Mobility* (London: Policy Studies Institute, 1990), 45.
16. J. Oppenheim, "What's Happening to Recess?" *Good Housekeeping*, September 1990, 66.
17. Hartle and Johnson refer to "mounting threats to recess period and playground time during the school day." See L. Hartle & J.E. Johnson, "Historical and Contemporary Influences on Outdoor Play Environments," in *Children on Playgrounds*, ed. C.H. Hart (Albany NY: SUNY Press, 1993), 14.
18. S.R. Kellert, introduction to *The Biophilia Hypothesis*, eds. S.R. Kellert & E.O. Wilson (Washington, DC: Island Press/Shearwater, 1993), 21.
19. Kellert, 20.
20. E.O. Wilson, "Biophilia and the Conservation Ethic," in *The Biophilia Hypothesis*, 31–32.

21. G.P. Nabhan & S. St. Antoine, "The Loss of Floral and Faunal Story: The Extinction of Experience," in *The Biophilia Hypothesis*, 229-50.

22. "Nostalgia and Odors," *Children's Environments* 9, no. 1 (1992): 13. See also the original report in A.R. Hirsch, "Nostalgia: A Neuropsychiatric Understanding," *Advances in Consumer Research* 19 (1992): 390–95.

23. D. Calabrese, introduction to *Creating a Sustainable Environment: Reversing a Legacy of Neglect* (Battle Creek, MI: Kellogg Foundation, 1990), 2.

24. H.R. Hungerford & T.L. Volk, "Changing Learner Behavior Through Environmental Education," *Journal of Environmental Education* 21, no. 3 (1991): 11.

25. R. Moore, *Childhood's Domain* (London: Croom Helm, 1986; reprint, Berkeley, CA: MIG Communications, 1990), 232.

26. Y.-F. Tuan, *Passing Strange and Wonderful* (Washington, DC: Island Press/Shearwater, 1993), 228.

27. F. Capra, *The Tao of Physics* (New York: Bantam, 1977).

28. See A.R. Olds, "From Cartwheels to Caterpillars: The Child's Need for Motion Outdoors," *Human Ecology Forum* 10 (winter 1980): 22–26.

29. M. Konner, Emory University professor of anthropology and psychiatry, says, "There is now an attempt to pathologize what was once considered the normal range of behavior of boys . . . . Today Tom Sawyer and Huckleberry Finn surely would have been diagnosed with both conduct disorder and ADHD," quoted in N. Angier, "The Debilitating Malady Called Boyhood," *New York Times*, 24 July 1994, sec. 4, 1, Northeast edition.

30. A. Olds, "Nature as Healer," *Children's Environments* 6 (spring 1989): 28.

31. A. Olds, "From Cartwheels to Caterpillars," 24.

32. W.A. Corsaro, *Friendship and Peer Culture in the Early Years* (Norwood, NJ: Ablex, 1985), 260.

33. N.J. Wagner, "Into the Woods" (masters thesis, University of Maryland Baltimore County, 1995), 102–3.

34. M. Lockheed & S. Klein, "Sex Equality in Classroom Organization and Climate," in *Handbook for Achieving Sex Equality through Education*, ed. S. Klein (Baltimore, MD: Johns Hopkins University Press, 1985), 263–84.

35. Corsaro, *Friendship and Peer Culture*, 193; quoting E. Goffman, *Asylums* (Garden City, NY: Doubleday, 1961), 320.

36. J.G. Magee, Jr., "High Flight," *New York Herald Tribune*, 8 February 1942.

Chapter 2, pages 17–34

1. J.L. Frost, "Reflections on Research and Practice in Outdoor Play Environments," *Dimensions of Early Childhood* 20, no. 4 (summer 1992): 7.

2. S. Kritchevsky & E. Prescott, *Planning Environments for Young Children: Physical Space*, 2nd ed. (Washington, DC: NAEYC, 1977), 7.

3. Kritchevsky & Prescott, 11–17.

4. A. Eriksen, *Playground Design: Outdoor Environments for Learning and Development* (New York: Van Nostrand Reinhold, 1985), 79–81.

5. M. Guddemi & A. Eriksen, "Designing Outdoor Learning Environments for and with Children," *Dimensions of Early Childhood* 20, no. 4 (summer 1992): 17–24.

6. The Houston Play Adventure Association hopes that others will join them in revitalizing the adventure playground movement that Americans experimented with somewhat in the 1970s, according to E.R. Shell in "Kids Don't Need Equipment, They Need Opportunity," *Smithsonian* 25 (July 1994): 79–87.

7. R. Moore, *Childhood's Domain* (London: Croom Helm, 1986; reprint, Berkeley, CA: MIG Communications, 1990), 241–42. Another plea for providing children with vegetation for play is M.A. Kirby's "Nature as Refuge in Children's Environments," *Children's Environments Quarterly* 6 (spring 1989): 7–12.

8. R.C. Moore, *Plants for Play: A Plant Selection Guide for Children's Outdoor Environments* (Berkeley, CA: MIG Communications, 1993).

9. L. Schneekloth observes that most adults perceive vegetation only as background, a perception that ignores our dependence on it. She asks, "If . . . very young children can experience plants differently before they are taught that plants are invisible, how can we facilitate and validate their more connective relationship? Surely this must be part of our mission in teaching our children about our home, Earth, and the perpetuation of all other species with which we share it." See her "Where Did You Go? The Forest. What Did You See? Nothing." *Children's Environments Quarterly* 6 (spring 1989): 17.

In a study of more than eight hundred 8- to 11-year-old children in England, M.R. Harvey found that children with more experience with vegetation showed more intellectual and aesthetic appreciation of the natural environment than did children with less experience. Experience included playing with, eating, working on vegetation (e.g., mowing the lawn); having it as an obstacle (e.g., allergies) or decorating with it; or having outdoor adventures (e.g., hiking or camping). Younger children reported more enjoyment of vegetation than did older children, a significant finding for primary teachers. See Harvey, "Children's Experiences with Vegetation," *Children's Environments Quarterly* 6 (spring 1989): 36–43.

10. E. Prescott, "Environment as Organizer in Child-Care Settings," in *Spaces for Children: The Built Environment and Child Development*, eds. C.S. Weinstein & T.G. David (New York: Plenum, 1987), 87.

11. S. Nicholson, "How Not to Cheat Children: The Theory of Loose Parts," *Landscape Architecture* 62 (October 1971): 30.

12. L.G. Shaw, "Designing Playgrounds for Able and Disabled Children," in *Spaces for Children*, 207–8.

13. J.D. Dempsey & J.L. Frost, "Play Environments in Early Childhood Education," in *Handbook of Research on the Education of Young Children*, ed. B. Spodek (New York: Macmillan, 1993), 315.

14. Using animals as a way to reach and teach difficult children is well known to teachers of young children. Research is slight in this area, but in one study including 9- to 15-year-old boys with both attention-deficit hyperactivity disorder (ADHD) and a variety of troubling behaviors, A. Katcher & G. Wilkins found that rules structured around the care of animals were accepted as rational when other social expectations were rejected as arbitrary and that speech and communication were facilitated by a program based on caring for animals. See Katcher & Wilkins, "Dialogue with Animals: Its Nature and Culture," in *The Biophilia Hypothesis*, eds. S.R. Kellert & E.O. Williams (Washington, DC: Island Press/Shearwater, 1993), 173–97. These researchers further note:
   The hyperactive children who were taught how to care for animals used that experience to learn biology and learn how to learn. They acquired method, fact, and a new moral orientation toward nature. If the curriculum was effective, it is because they were taught by people who cared for animals and nature and reflected that concern in their demeanor and instruction. Nature was not merely the subject matter; it was the world common to both teacher and student for which both had to assume responsibility. With that kind of teaching, the innate tendency to continue a dialogue with other kinds of life can be joined to the moral agenda of preserving that life. (193) Quoted by permission of the publisher.

15. This school is described in Y.B. Estes, "Environmental Education: Bringing Children and Nature Together," *Phi Delta Kappan* 74 (May 1993): special report K1–K12.

16. R.A. Hart, "Children's Participation in Planning and Design," in *Spaces for Children: The Built Environment and Child Development*, eds. C.S. Weinstein & T.G. David (New York: Plenum, 1987), 216–17.

17. Hart, 227–29. Other good descriptions of the participatory planning process are in S. Carr, M. Francis, L.G. Rivlin, & A. Stone, *Public Space* (New York: Cambridge University Press, 1992). Research analyzing the quality of children's participation is reported by L.G. Sheat & A.R. Beer, "Giving Pupils an Effective Voice in the Design and Use of Their Schools Grounds," in *Breaktime and the School: Understanding and Changing Playground Behaviour*, eds. P. Blatchford & S. Sharp (London & New York: Routledge, 1994), 90–106.

18. R.C. Moore describes the design process. See his "Before and After Asphalt: Diversity as an Ecological Measure of Quality in Children's Outdoor Environments," in *The Ecological Context of Children's Play*, eds. M.N. Bloch & A.D. Pellegrini (Norwood, NJ: Ablex, 1989), 191–213.

19. Eriksen, *Playground Design*, 66–82.

20. C. Ross & A. Ryan, "Changing Playground Society: A Whole-School Approach," in *Breaktime and the School*, 180–81.

21. Frost, "Reflections on Research and Practice," 10.

Chapter 3, pages 35–46

1. J. Dewey, "John Dewey on Education (1897)," in *Education in the United States: A Documentary History*, vol. 4, ed. S. Cohen (New York: Random House, 1974), 2213.

2. S. Humphries & S. Rowe, "The Biggest Classroom," in *Breaktime and the School: Understanding and Changing Playground Behaviour*, eds. P. Blatchford & S. Sharp (London & New York: Routledge, 1994), 110.

3. Coombes County Infant and Nursery School, "1993 Berkshire Environmental Action Award" (Coombes Infant School, School Road, Arborfield Cross, Reading, Berks, UK, 1993, photocopy), n.p.

4. Coombes School, "Action Award," n.p.

5. Humphries & Rowe, "The Biggest Classroom," 107–17.

6. P. Blatchford, *Playtime in the Primary School* (Windsor, UK: Nfer-Nelson, 1989), 98-105.

7. R. Mora, "The Creative Playground/Outdoor Learning Center," *Children's Environments Quarterly* 8, no. 1 (1991): 59. This description has many attractive photographs.

8. Personal conversation with Dr. Barbara Barlow, May 1993.

9. Mora, "The Creative Playground," 62.

10. S. Kornhauser quoted in T. Hiss & E. Koren, "Child's Play," *New Yorker* 69, no. 14 (24 May 1993): 78.

11. For a fuller description see N.R. Smith, "The Workyards of Sde Eliyahu: Places to Learn Resourcefulness," *Beginnings* 2, no. 2 (1985): 19–23.

12. B. Lucas, "Grounds for Change: Learning through Landscapes in Britain," *Children, Plants, and Gardens: Educational Opportunities—Proceedings from the AHS National Symposium, August 12-14, 1993, Chevy Chase, MD*, special issue of *American Horticulturalist* (July 1994), 9.

13. Lucas, "Grounds for Change," 8.

14. Lucas, 8. Butterfly gardens contain plants that butterflies favor for the nectar of the flowers or the leaves that their caterpillars eat. Math trails provide children with math activities, such as tree circumferences to measure or distances to pace. Sensory gardens contain plants that have distinctive textures, such as lamb's quarters; or tastes, such as watercress; or smells, such as various mints; or sounds, such as rustling grasses. A checkerboard garden has plantings arranged to resemble a checkerboard when looked at from above.

15. Lucas, 9.

16. B. Lucas, "Grounds for Change: The British Example" (speech presented at Out of the Classroom . . . Into the Garden: International Symposium on the Prepared Learning Environment, the Montessori Foundation and the American Horticultural Society, Arlington, Virginia, 8 August 1994).

17. M. Francis, "A Landscaper's Plea for Less Design," *American Horticulturist* (November 1993): 4

18. Evergreen Foundation publishes *The Guide to School Ground Naturalization: Welcoming Back the Wilderness* and a newsletter, *The Outdoor Classroom* (Evergreen Foundation, 355 Adelaide Street West, Suite 5A, Toronto, Ontario, M5V 1S3 Canada).

19. The Boston GreenSpace Alliance is located at 44 Bromfield Street, Boston, MA 02108.

20. Much information about creating "wildlife habitats" on school grounds comes from agencies traditionally involved with wildlife rather than schools: state and federal agencies for forestry, fish and game, agriculture, and natural resources. A wide array of programs are being sponsored; teachers might call one or more of the agencies in their area and ask what is being done for schools or might be started.

    Organizations that encourage habitat establishment are the National Wildlife Federation (1440 16th Street, Washington, DC 20036) and the National Institute for Urban Wildlife (P.O. Box 3015, Shepherdstown, WV 25443).

21. See J.M. Schaefer, D.W. Donelin, L.L. Linscott, & L. Cronin-Jones, *Schoolyard Ecosystems for Northeast Florida: A Guide for Planning, Installing, Maintaining and Using* (Gainesville, FL: University of Florida, n.d.). A guide for improving schoolyard wildlife habitats is available, plus information on state contacts, from the Project Wild national office (5430 Grosvenor Lane, Suite 230, Bethesda, MD, 20814-2142). The Institute for Ecosystem Studies, (Millbrook, NY 12545-0178) maintains a list of various schoolyard ecology projects in the United States and elsewhere.

22. Noting that the Persian word for garden is *paradise*, P. Shepard describes a Persian garden as an oasis in the desert, a walled enclosure with water, shade, and pleasing designs of flowers and other plants (the inspiration of Persian rugs). By contrast, in forested northern Europe an opening in the forest, originally a pasture where stock could graze, became a gathering place for communal activities. "It is an inverse oasis, an island of open space in the continuum of forest. In Old Saxon, 'paradise' was translated as 'meadow,'" describes Shepard, *Man In the Landscape* (College Station: Texas A&M University Press, 1991), 77.

    As we think about planning for children's outdoor space, both models of paradise inform us.

23. A. Martaurano, "The South Carolina Garden-Based Learning Network" (paper presented at Out of the Classroom . . . Into the Garden Symposium, 6 August 1994).

24. P. Ward, "A Child's Garden" (a presentation at Out of the Classroom . . . Into the Garden Symposium, 6 August 1994).

25. For a series of articles on therapeutic gardens, see *Landscape Architecture* 85, no. 1 (1995).

26. M.D. Lowe comments, "A major obstacle to growing food crops safely in many urban areas is the health threat from air, soil, or water contamination. Areas exposed to industrial emissions or air pollution from heavy traffic are generally inappropriate for growing food. Thoroughly washing grains, fruits and vegetables may remove airborne pollutants, but not soil- or waterborne lead and other heavy metals that have moved through the plant and concentrated in edible fruit, roots or leaves. Where agricultural extension is available, people can request a soil test to determine if their plots are safe. In mildly polluted areas, low levels of airborne dust and particulates can be screened by planting trees and other non-food plants around food crops." See her *Worldwatch Paper #105—Shaping Cities: The Environmental and Human Dimensions* (Washington, DC: Worldwatch Institute, 1991), 46–47. Quoted by permission.

27. R. Hart, "Fostering Earth Stewardship," *Children, Plants, and Gardens*, 5.

    Hart grew up in an environment of gardens and greenhouses because his parents ran a nursery near his school. Biographical notes at the end of his well-known *Children's Experience of Place* (New York: Irvington, 1979) reveal a child's view of this place.

    I often went there after school, working and playing until tea time. There were dozens of activities on the potting bench: using the hose for play with the soil under the bench while pretending to water the asparagus ferns; hunting and running from spiders in the box shed; caring for plants I had personally identified with; painting a door or a gate for my dad; exploring the tall weeds growing in the compost heaps at the back of the greenhouses; and dropping stones down the well. (490)

Hart's key phrase to remember, I think, is "working and playing," with perhaps an emphasis on playing.

28. C. Olwell, *Gardening from the Heart: Why Gardeners Garden* (Berkeley, CA: Antelope, 1990), 14.
29. J. Dighe, "Children and the Earth," *Young Children* 48 (March 1993): 59; quoting J. Cornell, *Sharing Nature with Children* (Nevada City, CA: Dawn, 1979), 11.
30. J. Dighe, "Children and the Earth," 59–60.
31. L. Chawla, "Out of the Garden and Into the World: Preparing Children to Care for the Earth" (speech presented at Out of the Classroom . . . Into the Garden Symposium, 5 August 1994).
32. Dighe, "Children and the Earth," 60.
33. B.-G. Holt, *Science with Young Children*, rev. ed (Washington, DC: NAEYC, 1989), 107.

Chapter 4, pages 47–56

1. This is a widely reported statistic. For example, see U.S. Public Interest Research Group (U.S.PIRG)/Consumer Federation of America (CFA), *Playing It Safe: The Second Nationwide Safety Survey of Public Playgrounds* (Washington, DC: U.S.PIRG and CFA, 1994), 1. T. Jambor and S.D. Palmer note that perhaps 200,000 children are injured enough to require some medical treatment, in *Playground Safety Manual* (Birmingham: University of Alabama Injury Prevention Research Center, 1991), ii.

   Playground deaths are relatively rare, about 17 per year. By contrast, for the 5- to 14-year-old child, "the chances of being killed at home or in the street as a pedestrian are roughly 47 to 63 times greater than the chance of being killed on a playground," according to A. Brett, R.C. Moore, & E.F. Provenzo, Jr., *The Complete Playground Book* (Syracuse, NY: Syracuse University Press, 1993), 149.
2. Jambor & Palmer, *Playground Safety Manual*, 4.
3. One recent survey of 443 playgrounds throughout the United States showed that 92% lacked adequate protective surfacing. Most playgrounds had shock-absorbent materials under some equipment but not all. See U.S. PIRG/CFA, *Playing It Safe*, 1.
4. J.L. Frost, *Play and Playscapes* (Albany NY: Delmar, 1992), 234–41.
5. U.S. Consumer Product Safety Commission (CPSC), *Handbook for Public Playground Safety*, 1991-305-724 (Washington, DC: Government Printing Office, 1991), 20–21.
6. Frost, *Play and Playscapes*, 227–33.
7. T. Jambor, "Required Reading on Outdoor Play Environments," *Dimensions of Early Childhood* 20, no. 4 (summer 1992): 39.
8. Frost, *Play and Playscapes*, 208.

9. See P. Blatchford, *Playtime in the Primary School* (Windsor, UK: Nfer-Nelson, 1989), for a full discussion of this problem in Britain.
10. S. Kritchevsky & E. Prescott, *Planning Environments for Young Children: Physical Space*, 2nd ed. (Washington, DC: NAEYC, 1977), 11–17.
11. Blatchford, *Playtime in the Primary School*, 81.
12. L. Schicker, "Design Criteria for Children and Wildlife in Residential Developments," in *Integrating Man and Nature in the Metropolitan Environment*, eds. L.W. Adams & D.L. Leedy (Columbia, MD: National Institute for Urban Wildlife, 1987), 102.
13. The Cooperative Extension Service, also known as the agricultural extension service or the extension service, originally provided farmers with advice and information. Currently, it educates citizens to apply research-based knowledge to critical issues facing individuals, families, and communities. Programs include the 4-H youth program, nutrition education for youth and adults, money management for youth, home and commercial horticulture, and education advice to farmers and commercial growers. The service in your area can be located in the government pages of the telephone book, variously under *A*, *C*, or *E*.
14. F. Wardle, "Bruderhof Education: Outdoor School," *Young Children* 50 (March 1995): 71.
15. R. Moore, S.M. Goltsman, & D.S. Iacofano, *Play for All Guidelines: Planning, Design, and Management of Outdoor Play Settings for All Children*, 2nd ed. (Berkeley, CA: MIG Communications, 1992), xii.

Chapter 5, pages 57–66

1. N. Angier writes that children's access to guns in this country makes us very wary of children's aggression and quick to label behavior as medical/psychological problems, which in another society (England is her example) would be accepted as within the range of normal behavior. See her "The Debilitating Malady Called Boyhood," *New York Times*, 24 July 1994, sec. 4, 16, Northeast edition.
2. H. Brun, "Floating vs. Stable Hierarchies," lecture at the University of Maryland Baltimore Campus, spring 1994.
3. C. McCarthy, "Why We Must Teach Peace," *Educational Leadership*, 50, no. 1 (1992), 8.
4. McCarthy, "Why We Must Teach Peace," 6–7.
5. R.G. Slaby, W.C. Roedell, D. Arezzo, & K. Hendrix, *Early Violence Prevention: Tools for Teachers of Young Children* (Washington, DC: NAEYC, 1995), provide research-based guidance for early childhood educators on how to help children develop nonviolent ways of solving problems. The authors list additional curriculum resources for violence prevention.

6. S. Wichert, *Keeping the Peace: Practicing Cooperation and Conflict Resolution with Preschoolers* (Philadelphia, PA: New Society, 1989).
7. M. Csikszentmihalyi, *The Evolving Self: A Psychology for the Third Millennium* (New York: HarperCollins, 1993).
8. G.S. Pettit & A.W. Harrist, "Children's Aggressive and Socially Unskilled Playground Behavior with Peers: Origins in Early Family Relations," in *Children on Playgrounds: Research Perspectives and Applications*, ed. C.H. Hart (Albany, NY: State University of New York Press, 1993), 240–70.
9. H.A. Murphy, J.M. Hutchison, & J. S. Bailey, "Behavioral School Psychology Goes Outdoors: The Effect of Organized Games on Playground Aggression," *Journal of Applied Behavior Analysis* 16, no. 1 (1983): 29–35.
10. I. Opie & P. Opie, *Children's Games in Street and Playground* (London: Oxford University Press, 1969).
11. R. Vignola & D. Vignola, *New York City Street Games: The Greatest Games Ever Played on Concrete* (Berkeley, CA: MIG Communications, 1993).
12. P. Blatchford cautions against both romanticizing traditional games and lamenting children's inability to play them. He observes that children continue to invent games based on contemporary life, e.g., superhero play. See his *Playtime in the Primary School* (Windsor, UK: Nfer-Nelson, 1989), 12–18.
13. According to anthropologists J.M. Roberts and B. Sutton-Smith, the games we play reflect our culture's values. See their "Child Training and Game Involvement," *Ethnology* 1 (1962): 166–85. Although a large part of teaching is transmitting traditional values, surely the values that seem shopworn ought not be transmitted through games we deliberately teach.
14. M.K. Clayton, "Peace on the Playground: Teaching Care, Friendliness, and Cooperation," *A Newsletter for Teachers* 4, no. 2 (1992): 3–5.
15. D. Olweus, "Bullies on the Playground: The Role of Victimization," in *Children on Playgrounds*, 85–125.
16. Olweus, "Bullies on the Playground," 124.
17. L.G. Katz, D. Evangelou, & J.A. Hartman, *The Case for Mixed-Age Grouping in Early Education* (Washington, DC: NAEYC, 1990).
18. Blatchford, *Playtime in the Primary School*, 108–15.
19. K. Fry-Miller & J. Myers-Wall, *Young Peacemakers Project Book* (Elgin, IL: Brethren, 1988), 6.
20. B. Thorne, *Gender Play: Girls and Boys in School* (New Brunswick, NJ: Rutgers University Press, 1993), 173.

Chapter 6, pages 67–78

1. S. Gaster, "Historical Changes in Children's Access to U.S. Cities: A Critical Review," *Children's Environments* 9, no. 2 (1992): 34.
2. American Greenways Program, "Fact Sheet No. 2" (Arlington, VA: The Conservation Fund, n.d), n.p.
   Fact sheets on various aspects of the greenways movement, including a bibliography and a list of active organizations, may be obtained from The Conservation Fund, 1800 North Kent Street, Suite 1120, Arlington, VA 22209; 703-525-6300, Fax 703-525-4610. See also from The Conservation Fund, C.A. Flink & R.M. Stearns, *Greenways: A Guide to Planning, Design, and Development* (Washington, DC: Island Press/Shearwater, 1993).
3. President's Commission on Americans Outdoors, *Report and Recommendations to the President of the United States* (Washington, DC: Government Printing Office, 1987); and National Trails Agenda Project U.S., *Trails for All Americans: The Report of the National Trails Agenda Project* (Washington, DC: National Park Service, U.S. Department of Interior, 1990).
4. U.S. Department of Transportation (DOT), *A Summary of Intermodal Surface Transportation Efficiency Act of 1991*, #FHWA-PL-92-008 (Washington, DC: DOT, 1992).
5. A. Lusk, "Let's Build 108,000 New Garden Classrooms for Children," *Children, Plants, and Gardens: Educational Opportunities—Proceedings from AHS National Symposium, August 12–14, 1993, Chevy Chase, MD*, special issue of *American Horticulturist* (July 1994): 34–35.
6. A. Lusk, personal communication, August 1994.
7. An information packet on the program may be obtained for a nominal amount from the National Wildlife Federation, 1-800-432-6564.
8. S. Stein, *Noah's Garden* (Boston: Houghton Mifflin, 1993), 252.
9. Stein, *Noah's Garden*, 254.
10. For examples, see M.D. Lowe, *Worldwatch Paper #105—Shaping Cities: The Environmental and Human Dimensions* (Washington, DC: Worldwatch Institute, 1991).
11. The Urban Forestry Program, funded at $28 million in 1994, provides monies to each state forester that are available as grants to communities and organizations to plant trees. The aim is to improve the quality of life in cities and towns. Another Forest Service program, the Urban Resource Partnership, is currently providing funds to Seattle, Chicago, and Atlanta to promote planting and taking care of trees. Teachers can contact their state forester to learn what projects are occurring in their state and how their schools might be involved. State foresters are typically in Departments of

Natural Resources, although each state has its own organizational structure.

12. For information on the project, see the brochure *Revitalizing Baltimore: Restoring Our Environment, Restoring Our Communities* (Baltimore: Parks and Recreation Department, 1994).

13. *Public Space for Public Life: A Plan for the Twenty-first Century* (New York: The Parks Council and Central Park Conservancy, December 1993). Quoted by permission. © The Parks Council and Central Park Conservancy.

14. *Public Space for Public Life*, 39.

15. *Public Space for Public Life*, 37.

16. *Public Space for Public Life*, 59.

17. The policy paper was issued in December. By June, a new mayor proposed a 23% cut in the number of full-time employees, following a 28% cut over the previous three years. See L. Davidoff, "Field of Broken Dreams," *New York Times*, 18 June 1994, 15, Northeast edition.

18. The President's Commission on Americans Outdoors, *Report and Recommendations*, 99.

19. R.L. Thayer, Jr., *Gray World, Green Heart: Technology, Nature, and the Sustainable Landscape* (New York: John Wiley, 1994).

20. M. Francis, "Children's Use of Open Space in Village Homes," *Children's Environments Quarterly* 1, (winter 1984/85): 36–38.

21. Francis, "Children's Use of Open Space," 37.

22. J. Kastner, "My Empty Lot," *New York Times Magazine*, 10 October 1993, 44.

23. M.D. Lowe, "Reclaiming Cities for People," *World Watch* 5 (July/August 1992): 20.

24. R.C. Moore, *Childhood's Domain* (London: Croom Helm, 1986; reprint, Berkeley, CA: MIG Communications, 1990), 238.

25. B. Eubank-Ahrens, "The Impact of *Woonerven* on Children's Behavior," *Children's Environments Quarterly* 1 (winter 1984/85): 39–45.

Chapter 7, pages 79–81

1. B.B. Whiting & C.P. Edwards, *Children of Different Worlds* (Cambridge, MA: Harvard University Press, 1988).

2. W. Titman, *Special Places; Special People: The Hidden Curriculum of School Grounds* (Goldaming, Surrey, UK: World Wide Fund for Nature/Learning Through Landscapes, 1994), 25–27.

Featured quotations, throughout the book

p. vi—L. Thomas, *Lives of a Cell* (New York: Viking\Penguin, 1974). Reprinted by permission.

p. 8—J. St. Giermaine, speech presented at Out of the Classroom . . . Into the Garden: International Symposium on the Prepared Learning Environment, the Montessori Foundation and the American Horticultural Society, Arlington, Virginia, 4–7 August 1994.

p. 9—B. Pettit, on-line conversation on outdoor play, the America Tomorrow Online Center® Early Childhood Bulletin Board on PRODIGY® (formerly ATLIS), 17 June 1994.

p. 14—A. Welch, speech at "Revitalizing Baltimore" Conference, Baltimore, Maryland, 25 June 1994.

p. 20—S. Goltsman, quoted by M. Leccese in "Redefining the Idea of Play," *Landscape Architecture* 84 (October 1994): 15.

p. 26—N. Alexander, J. Chapman, & J. Bilmes, on-line conversation on outdoor play, the America Tomorrow Online Center® Early Childhood Bulletin Board on PRODIGY® (formerly ATLIS), 28-29 June 1994.

p. 27—D. Sobel, *Children's Special Places* (Tucson, AZ: Zephyr, 1993).

p. 28—P. Warfield, "Back Yard," n.p., n.d. Reprinted by permission. © Pamela Warfield.

p. 31—E.B. White, *Charlotte's Web* (New York: Harper & Row, 1952), 176.

p. 41—J. Cornell, *Sharing Nature with Children* (Nevada City, CA: Dawn, 1979), 11.

p. 52—F. Wallach, "What Did We Do Wrong?" *Parks and Recreation* 27 (April 1992): 56.

p. 53—P. Flohr, personal communication, Anne Arundel County, Maryland, 10 July 1995.

p. 60—R.L. Stevenson, "Good and Bad Children," *A Child's Garden of Verses* (1885; reprint, New York: Delacorte, 1985).

p. 61—M. Montessori, *Education and Peace*, trans. (Chicago: Henry Regnery, 1972); originally published as *Educazione e Pace* (Italy: Garzanti Editore, 1949).

p. 65—S. Humphries, personal communication, 2 August 1995.

p. 67—*Public Space for Public Life: A Plan for the Twenty-first Century* (New York: The Parks Council and Central Park Conservancy, December 1993), 7.

p. 70—W. Williams quoted in W. Poole & S. Ives, "Building Hope in America's Cities," *Land and People* 5 (fall 1993): 4.

p. 75—R.L. Thayer, *Gray World, Green Heart: Technology, Nature, and the Sustainable Landscape* (New York: John Wiley, 1994), 302-6. Reprinted by permission.

p. 79—L. Standing Bear, *Land of the Spotted Eagle* (Lincoln: University of Nebraska Press, 1933), 45; quoted in E.O. Wilson & S. Kellert, eds., *The Biophilia Hypothesis* (Washington, DC: Island Press/Shearwater, 1993), 54.

p. 106—J.L. Frost, *Play and Playscapes* (Albany, NY: Delmar, 1992), 106. Reproduced by permission. © 1992 Delmar Publishers.

Selected Bibliography

Baltimore Parks and Recreation Department. *Revitalizing Baltimore: Restoring Our Environment, Restoring Our Communities.* Baltimore, MD: Author, 1994.

Blakely, K., M.A. Lang, & R. Hart. *Getting in Touch with Play: Creating Play Environments for Children with Visual Impairments.* New York: Lighthouse for the Blind, 1991.

Blatchford, P. *Playtime in the Primary School.* Windsor, UK: Nfer-Nelson, 1989.

Blatchford, P., & S. Sharp, eds. *Breaktime and the School: Understanding and Changing Playground Behaviour.* London & New York: Routledge, 1994.

Brett, A., R.C. Moore, & E.F. Provenzo, Jr. *The Complete Playground Book.* Syracuse, NY: Syracuse University Press, 1993.

Calabrese, D. Introduction to *Creating a Sustainable Environment: Reversing a Legacy of Neglect.* Battle Creek, MI: Kellogg Foundation, 1990.

Carr, S., M. Francis, L.G. Rivlin, & A. Stone. *Public Space.* New York: Cambridge University Press, 1992.

Clayton, M.K. "Peace on the Playground: Teaching Care, Friendliness, and Cooperation." *A Newsletter for Teachers* 4, no. 2 (1992).

Cobb, E. *The Ecology of Imagination in Childhood.* New York: Columbia University Press, 1977.

Cornell, J. *Sharing Nature with Children.* Nevada City, CA: Dawn, 1979.

Corsaro, W.A. *Friendship and Peer Culture in the Early Years.* Norwood, NJ: Ablex, 1985.

Csikszentmihalyi, M. *The Evolving Self: A Psychology for the Third Millennium.* New York: HarperCollins, 1993.

Dargan, A., & S. Zeitlin. *City Play.* New Brunswick, NJ: Rutgers University Press, 1990.

Dempsey, J.D., & J.L. Frost. "Play Environments in Early Childhood Education." In *Handbook of Research on the Education of Young Children,* ed. B. Spodek. New York: Macmillan, 1993.

Dighe, J. "Children and the Earth." *Young Children* 48 (March 1993).

Eriksen, A. *Playground Design: Outdoor Environments for Learning and Development.* New York: Van Nostrand Reinhold, 1985.

Estes, Y. B. "Environmental Education: Bringing Children and Nature Together." *Phi Delta Kappan* 74 (May 1993, Special Report).

Eubank-Ahrens, B. "The Impact of *Woonerven* on Children's Behavior." *Children's Environments Quarterly* 1 (winter 1984/85).

Fink, D.B. "School-Age Child Care: Where the Spirit of Neighborhood Lives." *Children's Environments Quarterly* 3 (summer 1986): 9-11.

Flink, C.A., & R.M.Stearns. *Greenways: A Guide to Planning, Design, and Development.* Washington, DC: Island Press/Shearwater, 1993.

Francis, M. "Children's Use of Open Space in Village Homes." *Children's Environments Quarterly* 1 (winter 1984/85).

Frost, J.L. *Play and Playscapes.* Albany NY: Delmar, 1992.

Frost, J.L. "Reflections on Research and Practice in Outdoor Play Environments." *Dimensions of Early Childhood* 20, no. 4 (summer 1992).

Fry-Miller, K. & J. Myers-Wall. *Young Peacemakers Project Book.* Elgin, IL: Brethren, 1988.

Gaster, S. "Historical Changes in Children's Access to U.S. Cities: A Critical Review." *Children's Environments* 9, no. 2 (1992).

Goltsman, S.M., T.A. Gilbert, & S. D. Wohlford. *The Accessibility Checklist: An Evaluation System for Buildings and Outdoor Settings.* 2nd ed. Berkeley, CA: MIG Communications, 1993.

Guddemi, M., & A. Eriksen. "Designing Outdoor Learning Environments for and with Children." *Dimensions of Early Childhood* 20, no. 4 (summer 1992).

Hart, R. *Children's Experience of Place.* New York: Irvington, 1979.

Hart, R.A. "Children's Participation in Planning and Design." In *Spaces for Children: The Built Environment and Child Development,* eds. C.S. Weinstein & T.G. David. New York: Plenum, 1987.

Hart, R. "Fostering Earth Stewardship," *Children, Plants, and Gardens: Proceedings from the AHS national Symposium, August 12-14, 1993, Chevy Chase, MD,* special issue *American Horticulturist,* July, 1994.

Hartle, L., & J.E. Johnson. "Historical and Contemporary Influences on Outdoor Play Environments." In *Children on Playgrounds,* ed. C.H. Hart. Albany, NY: SUNY Press, 1993.

Harvey, M.R. "Children's Experiences with Vegetation." *Children's Environments Quarterly* 6 (spring 1989).

Hillman, M, & J.G.U. Adams. "Children's Freedom and Safety." *Children's Environments* 9, no. 2 (1992).

Hillman, M., J. Adams, & J. Whitelegg. *One False Move . . . : A Study of Children's Independent Mobility.* London: Policy Studies Institute, 1990.

Hiss, T., & E. Koren. "Child's Play." *New Yorker* 69, 24 May 1993.

Holt, B.-G. *Science with Young Children.* Rev. ed. Washington, DC: NAEYC, 1989.

Humphries, S., & S. Rowe. "The Biggest Classroom." In *Breaktime and the School: Understanding and Changing Playground Behaviour,* eds. P. Blatchford & S. Sharp. London & New York: Routledge, 1994.

Hungerford, H.R., & T.L. Volk. "Changing Learner Behavior Through Environmental Education." *Journal of Environmental Education* 21, no. 3 (1991).

Jambor, T. "Required Reading on Outdoor Play Environments." *Dimensions of Early Childhood* 20 (summer 1992).

Jambor, T., & S.D. Palmer. Introduction to *Playground Safety Manual.* Birmingham, AL: University of Alabama Injury Prevention Research Center, 1991.

Katcher, A., & G. Wilkins. "Dialogue with Animals: Its Nature and Culture." In *The Biophilia Hypothesis,* eds. S.R. Kellert & E.O. Wilson. Washington, DC: Island Press/Shearwater, 1993.

Kellert, S.R. Introduction to *The Biophilia Hypothesis,* eds. S.R. Kellert & E.O. Wilson. Washington, DC: Island Press/Shearwater, 1993.

Kirby, M. "Nature as Refuge in Children's Environments." *Children's Environments Quarterly* 6 (spring 1989).

Kritchevsky, S., & E. Prescott. *Planning Environments for Young Children: Physical Space.* 2nd ed. Washington, DC: NAEYC, 1977.

Leccese, M. "Redefining the Idea of Play." *Landscape Architecture* 84 (October 1994).

Lindgren, H. "Grassroots Security." *Landscape Architecture* 85 (February 1995).

Louv, R. "The Nature of Childhood." In *Childhood's Future.* Boston: Houghton Mifflin, 1990.

Lowe, M.D. *Worldwatch Paper #5—Shaping Cities: The Environmental and Human Dimensions.* Washington, DC: Worldwatch Institute, 1991.

Lowe, M.D. "Reclaiming Cities for People." *World Watch* 5 (July/August 1992).

Lucas, B. "Grounds for Change: Learning through Landscapes in Britain." *Children, Plants, and Gardens: Proceedings from the AHS National Symposium, August 12-14, 1993, Chevy Chase, MD,* special issue *American Horticulturalist* (July 1994).

Lusk, A. "Let's Build 108,000 New Garden Classrooms for Children." *Children, Plants, and Gardens: Educational Opportunities—Proceedings from AHS National Symposium, August 12-14, 1993, Chevy Chase, MD,* special issue of *American Horticulturist* (July 1994).

McCarthy, C. "Why We Must Teach Peace." *Educational Leadership* 50 (September 1992).

Moore, R.C. "Before and After Asphalt: Diversity as an Ecological Measure of Quality in Children's Outdoor Environments." In *The Ecological Context of Children's Play,* eds. M.N. Bloch & A.D. Pellegrini. Norwood, NJ: Ablex, 1989.

Moore, R. *Childhood's Domain.* London: Croom Helm, 1986. Reprint, Berkeley, CA: MIG Communications, 1990.

Moore, R.C. "Streets as Playgrounds." In *Public Streets for Public Use,* ed. A.V. Moudon. New York: Columbia University Press, 1991.

Moore, R.C. *Plants for Play: A Plant Selection Guide for Children's Outdoor Environments.* Berkeley, CA: MIG Communications, 1993.

Moore, R.C., S.M. Goltsman, & D.S. Iacofano, eds. *Play for All Guidelines: Planning, Design and Management of Outdoor Play Settings for All Children,* 2nd ed. Berkeley, CA: MIG Communications, 1992.

Mora, R. "The Creative Playground/Outdoor Learning Center." *Children's Environments Quarterly* 8, no.1 (1991).

Murphy, H.A., J. M. Hutchison, & J.S. Bailey. "Behavioral School Psychology Goes Outdoors: The Effect of Organized Games on Playground Aggression." *Journal of Applied Behavior Analysis* 16 (spring 1983).

Nabhan, G.P., & S. St. Antoine. "The Loss of Floral and Faunal Story: The Extinction of Experience." In *The Biophilia Hypothesis,* eds. S.R. Kellert & E.O. Wilson. Washington, DC: Island Press/Shearwater, 1993.

National Trails Agenda Project. *Trails for All Americans: The Report of the National Trails Agenda Project.* Washington, DC: National Park Service, U.S. Department of Interior, 1990.

Nicholson, S. "How Not to Cheat Children: The Theory of Loose Parts." *Landscape Architecture* 62 (October 1971).

Olds, A.R. "From Cartwheels to Caterpillars: The Child's Need for Motion Outdoors." *Human Ecology Forum* 10 (winter 1980).

Olds, A.R. "Nature as Healer." *Children's Environments* 6 (spring 1989).

Olwell, C. *Gardening from the Heart: Why Gardeners Garden.* Berkeley, CA: Antelope, 1990.

Olweus, D. "Bullies on the Playground: The Role of Victimization." In *Children on Playgrounds: Research Pespectives and Applications.* Albany: State University of New York Press, 1993.

Opie, I., & P. Opie. *Children's Games in Street and Playground.* London: Oxford University Press, 1969.

Oppenheim, J. "What's Happening to Recess?" *Good Housekeeping,* September 1990.

The Parks Council and Central Park Conservancy. *Public Space for Public Life: A Plan for the Twenty-first Century*. New York: The Parks Council and Central Park Conservancy, 1993.

Pettit, G.S., & A.W. Harrist. "Children's Aggressive and Socially Unskilled Playground Behavior With Peers: Origins in Early Family Relations." In *Children on Playgrounds: Research Perspectives and Applications*. Albany: State University of New York Press, 1993.

Prescott, E. "Environment as Organizer in Child-Care Settings." In *Spaces for Children: The Built Environment and Child Development*, eds. C. Weinstein & T.G. David. New York: Plenum, 1987.

Roberts, J.M., & B. Sutton-Smith. "Child Training and Game Involvement." *Ethnology* 1 (1962).

Ross, C., & A. Ryan. "Changing Playground Society: A Whole-School Approach." In *Breaktime and the School: Understanding and Changing School Behaviour*, eds. P. Blatch-ford & S. Sharp. London & New York: Routledge, 1994.

Schaefer, J. M., D.W. Donelin, L.L. Linscott, & L. Cronin-Jones. *Schoolyard Ecosystems for Northeast Florida: A Guide for Planning, Installing, Maintaining and Using*. Gainesville, FL: University of Florida, n.d.

Schicker, L. "Design Criteria for Children and Wildlife in Residential Developments." *Integrating Man and Nature in the Metropolitan Environment*, eds. L.W. Adams & D.L. Leedy. Columbia, MD: National Institute for Urban Wildlife, 1987.

Schneekloth, L. "Where Did You Go? The Forest. What Did You See? Nothing." *Children's Environments Quarterly* 6 (spring 1989).

Shaw, L.G. "Designing Playgrounds for Able and Disabled Children." In *Spaces for Children: The Built Environment and Child Development*, eds. C.S. Weinstein & T.G. David. New York: Plenum, 1987.

Sheat, L.G., & A.R. Beer. "Giving Pupils an Effective Voice in the Design and Use of Their Schools Grounds." In *Breaktime and the School: Understanding and Changing Playground Behaviour*, eds. P. Blatchford & S. Sharp. London & New York: Routledge, 1994.

Shell, E.R. "Kids Don't Need Equipment, They Need Opportunity." *Smithsonian* 25 (July 1994).

Shepard, P. *Man In the Landscape*. College Station: Texas A&M University Press, 1991.

Slaby, R.G., W.C. Roedell, D. Arezzo, & K. Hendrix. *Early Violence Prevention: Tools for Teachers of Young Children*. Washington, DC: NAEYC, 1995.

Smith, N.R. "The Workyards of Sde Eliyahu: Places to Learn Resourcefulness." *Beginnings* 2, no. 2 (1985).

Stein, S. *Noah's Garden*. Boston: Houghton Mifflin, 1993.

Thayer, Jr., R.L. *Gray World, Green Heart: Technology, Nature, and the Sustainable Landscape*. New York: John Wiley, 1994.

Thorne, B. *Gender Play: Girls and Boys in School*. New Brunswick, NJ: Rutgers University Press, 1993.

Titman, W. *Special Places, Special People: The Hidden Curriculum of School Grounds*. Goldaming, Surrey, UK: World Wide Fund for Nature/Learning Through Landscapes, 1994.

Tuan, Y.-F. *Passing Strange and Wonderful*. Washington, DC: Island Press/Shearwater, 1993.

U.S. Consumer Product Safety Commission. *Handbook for Public Playground Safety*. Washington DC: U.S. Government Printing Office, 1991.

U.S. Department of Transportation. *A Summary of Intermodal Surface Transportation Efficiency Act of 1991*. #FHWA-PL-92-008. Washington, DC: U.S. Department of Transportation, 1992.

U.S. Public Interest Research Group (U.S. PIRG), & Consumer Federation of America (CFA). *Playing It Safe: The Second Nationwide Safety Survey of Public Playgrounds*. Washington, DC: U.S. PIRG and CFA, 1994.

Vignola, R., & D. Vignola. *New York City Street Games: The Greatest Games Ever Played on Concrete*. Berkeley, CA: MIG Communications, 1993.

Wagner, N.J. "Into the Woods," unpublished masters thesis, University of Maryland Baltimore County, 1995.

Wardle, F. "Bruderhof Education: Outdoor School." *Young Children* 50 (March 1995).

Whiting, B.B., & C.P. Edwards. *Children of Different Worlds*. Cambridge, MA: Harvard University Press, 1988.

Wichert, S. *Keeping the Peace: Practicing Co-operation and Conflict Resolution with Pre-schoolers*. Philadelphia, PA: New Society, 1989.

Wilson, E.O. "Biophilia and the Conservation Ethic." In *The Biophilia Hypothesis*, eds. S.R. Kellert & E.O. Wilson. Washington, DC: Island Press/Shearwater, 1993.

Wyzga, M. *Homes for Wildlife: A Planning Guide for Enchancement on School Grounds*. Concord, NH: New Hampshire Fish and Game Department, n.d.

Appendix A
Useful Books

Outdoor Play

Adams, E. *Learning Through Landscapes: A Report on the Use, Design, Management and Development of School Grounds.* Winchester, Hants, UK: Learning Through Landscapes Trust, 1990.

Baker, K.R. *Let's Play Outdoors.* Washington, DC: NAEYC, 1991 (1965).

Bengtsson, A. *Environmental Planning for Children.* New York: Praeger, 1970.

Brett, A., R.C. Moore, & E.F. Provenzo, Jr. *The Complete Playground Book.* Syracuse, NY: Syracuse University Press, 1993.

Cohen, U., A.B. Hill, C.G. Lane, T. McGinty, & G.T. Moore. *Recommendations for Child Play Areas.* Milwaukee, WI: Center for Architecture and Urban Planning, University of Wisconsin–Milwaukee, 1979.

Dargan, A., & S. Zeitlin. *City Play.* Brunswick, NJ: Rutgers University Press, 1990.

Ellison, G. *Play Structures.* Pasadena, CA: Pacific Oaks College, 1974.

Eriksen, A. *Playground Design.* New York: Van Nostrand Reinhold, 1985.

Frost, J.L. *Play and Playscapes.* Albany, NY: Delmar, 1992.

Frost, J.L., & B.L. Klein. *Children's Play and Playgrounds.* Boston, MA: Allyn & Bacon, 1979.

Greenman, J. *Caring Spaces, Learning Places: Children's Environments That Work.* Redmond, WA: Exchange, 1988.

Hart, C.H., ed. *Children on Playgrounds: Research Perspectives and Applications.* Albany: State University of New York, 1993.

Hogan, P. *The Nuts and Bolts of Playground Construction.* West Point, NY: Leisure, 1982.

Kosanke, N., & N. Warner. *Creative Play Areas: Simple, Inexpensive Projects Parents and Children Can Do Together.* Nephi, UT: Innovation Station, 1990.

Kritchevsky, S., & E. Prescott. *Planning Environments for Young Children.* Washington, DC: NAEYC, 1977.

Moore, R.C., & H.H. Wong. *Natural Learning: The Story of the Washington School Environmental Yard.* Berkeley, CA: MIG Communications, in press.

Moore, R.C., S.M. Goltsman, & D.S. Iacofano, eds. *Play for All Guidelines, Second Edition: Planning, Design and Management of Outdoor Play Settings for All Children.* Berkeley, CA: MIG Communications, 1992.

Titman, W. *Special Places; Special People: The Hidden Curriculum of School Grounds.* Goldaming, Surrey, UK: World Wide Fund for Nature/Learning Through Landscapes, 1994.

Playground Games

Gregson, B. *The Outrageous Outdoor Games Book.* Carthage, IL: Fearon, 1984.

Kamii, C., & R. DeVries. *Group Games in Early Education: Implications of Piaget's Theory.* Washington, DC: NAEYC, 1980.

Orlick, T. *The Cooperative Sports and Games Book* and *The Second Cooperative Sports and Games Book.* New York: Pantheon, 1978, 1982.

Rowe, S., & S. Humphries. *Playing Around: Activities and Exercises for Social and Cooperative Learning.* London: Forbes, 1994.

Sobel, J. *Everybody Wins: 393 Non-Competitive Games for Young Children.* New York: Walker, 1983.

Plants and Gardens

This list is adapted by permission, from C. Wiseman, Books for Growing a Garden, and M. Heffernan, Key Gardening Books for Children, in "Children, Plants, and Gardens: Educational Opportunities," *American Horticulturalist* (July 1994): 38–40. © American Horticultural Society.

For Children

Bjork, C. *Linnea's Windowsill Garden.* Pownal, VT: Storey, 1978.

Bunting, E. *Flower Garden.* San Diego, CA: Harcourt, 1994.

Carle, E. *The Tiny Seed.* Saxonville, MA: Picture Book Studio, 1987.

Caseley, J. *Grandpa's Garden Lunch.* New York: Greenwillow/William Morrow, 1990.

Cooney, B. *Miss Rumphius.* New York: Viking, 1982.

Creasey, R. *Blue Potatoes, Orange Tomatoes.* New York: Little Brown/Sierra Club, 1994.

Ehlert, L. *Planting a Rainbow.* San Diego, CA: Harcourt, 1988.

Ehlert, L. *Growing Vegetable Soup.* San Diego, CA: Harcourt, 1989.

Florian, D. *Vegetable Garden.* San Diego, CA: Harcourt, 1991.

Gibbons, G. *From Seed to Plant.* New York: Holiday, 1991.

Heller, R. *The Reason for a Flower.* New York: Grosset, 1983.

Jordan, H. *How a Seed Grows,* rev. ed. New York: HarperCollins, 1992.

Kelly, M.A. *A Child's Book of Wildflowers.* New York: Four Winds/Macmillan, 1992.

Kraus, R. *The Carrot Seed.* New York: Harper & Row, 1945.

Kuhn, D. *More Than Just a Vegetable Garden.* Columbus, OH: Silver/Paramount, 1992.

Lauber, P. *Seeds Pop, Stick, Glide.* New York: Crown/Random House, 1981.

Lobel, A. *Alison's Zinnia.* New York: Greenwillow/William Morrow, 1990.

Maestro, B. *How Do Apples Grow?* New York: HarperCollins, 1992.

Moncure, J.B. *How Seeds Travel: Popguns and Parachutes.* Chicago: Children's Press, 1990.

Muller, G. *The Garden in the City.* New York: Dutton, 1992.

Robbins, K. *A Flower Grows.* New York: Dial, 1990.

Seymour, P. *How Things Grow.* New York: Dutton, 1988.

Steele, M.Q. *Anna's Garden Songs.* New York: Greenwillow/William Morrow, 1989.

Thomas, E. *Green Beans.* Minneapolis, MN: Carolrhoda, 1992.

Titherington, J. *Pumpkin, Pumpkin.* New York: Greenwillow/William Morrow, 1986.

Wexler, J. *Flowers, Fruits, Seeds.* Englewood Cliffs, NJ: Prentice Hall, 1987.

Wiesner, D. *June 29, 1999.* Boston: Clarion/Houghton Mifflin, 1992.

Wilkes, A. *My First Garden Book.* New York: Grosset, 1992.

Williams, V.B. *Cherries and Cherry Pits.* New York: Greenwillow/William Morrow, 1986.

Wilner, I. *A Garden Alphabet.* New York: Dutton, 1991.

Wilson, S. *Muskrat, Muskrat, Eat Your Peas!* New York: Simon & Schuster, 1989.

For Teachers

Appel, G., & R. Jaffe. *The Growing Classroom: Garden-Based Science.* Reading, MA: Addison-Wesley, 1990.

Brooklyn Botanic Garden. *Gardening with Children: A Handbook.* Brooklyn: Brooklyn Botanic Garden Press, 1984.

Hunken, J. *Botany for All Ages: Learning About Nature Through Activities Using Plants.* Old Saybrook, CT: Globe Pequot, 1989.

Jekyl, G. *Children and Gardens.* Wappinger Falls, NY: Antique Collector's Club, 1982.

Jeunesse, G., & P. de Bourgoing. *Fruit.* New York: Cartwheel/Scholastic, 1991.

Lovejoy, S. *Sunflower Houses.* Loveland, CO: Interweave, 1991.

MacLatchie, S. *Gardening with Kids.* Emmaus, PA: Rodale, 1977.

Ocone, L., with E. Pranis. *The National Gardening Association Guide to Kids' Gardening: A Complete Guide for Teachers, Parents, and Youth Leaders.* New York: John Wiley & Sons, 1990.

Project Wild. *Project Wild Elementary Activity Guide,* rev. ed. Boulder, CO: Project Wild/Western Regional Environmental Education Council, 1986.

Tilgner, L. *Let's Grow! 72 Gardening Adventures with Children.* Pownal, VT: Storey, 1988.

Waters, M. *The Victory Garden Kid's Book.* Boston: Houghton Mifflin, 1988.

Outdoor Activities

American Horticultural Society. *Children, Plants, and Gardens: Educational Opportunities: Proceedings from the AHS National Symposium, August 12 to 14, 1993, Chevy Chase, Maryland.* Special issue of *American Horticulturist*, July 1994.

    Forms an extremely useful compilation of outstanding garden projects, including information on how to contact individuals who are resources. It provides bibliographies and lists of organizations involved with youth gardening. Two of the bibliographies on children's books and teacher resources, amended in this Appendix under the heading "Plants and Gardens," provide an entry into the extensive literature on this subject.

Connect: K-8 Hands-On Science and Math Across the Curriculum (bimonthly newsletter published since 1987). Brattleboro, VT: Teachers' Laboratory.

Cornell, J. *Sharing Nature with Children.* Nevada City, CA: Dawn, 1979.

Cornell, J. *Sharing the Joy of Nature.* Nevada City, CA: Dawn, 1989.

Herman, M.L., A.L. Schimpf, J.F. Passineau, & P. Treuer. *Teaching Kids to Love the Earth.* Duluth, MN: Pfeifer-Hamilton, 1991.

Holt, B.-G. *Science with Young Children—Revised Edition.* Washington, DC: NAEYC, 1989.

Katz, A. *Naturewatch: Exploring Nature with Your Children.* Reading, MA: Addison-Wesley, 1986.

Kohl, M.F., & C. Gainer. *Good Earth Art: Environmental Art for Kids.* Bellingham, WA: Bright Ring, 1991.

McIntyre, M. *Early Childhood and Science.* Washington, DC: National Science Teachers Association, 1984.

Nicklesburg, J. *Nature Activities for Early Childhood.* Menlo Park, CA: Addison-Wesley, 1976.

Project Learning Tree. *Environmental Education Pre K-8 Activity Guide.* Washington, DC: Project, 1993.

Project Wild. *Project Wild Elementary Activity Guide.* Boulder, CO: Project Wild/Western Regional Environmental Education Council, 1986.

Redleaf, R. *Open the Door, Let's Explore: Neighborhood Field Trips for Young Children.* St. Paul, MN: Toys 'n' Things, 1983.

Russell, H.R. *Ten-Minute Field Trips.* Chicago: J.G. Ferguson, 1973. Reprint, Washington, DC: National Science Teachers Association, 1993.

Wilke, R.J., ed. *Environmental Education Teacher Resource Handbook: A Practical Guide for K-12 Environmental Education.* Milwood, NY: Kraus International, 1993. (Also available through National Science Teachers Association.)

Learning through Landscapes

Adams, E. *Learning Through Landscapes.* Winchester, Hants, UK: Learning Through Landscapes Trust, 1990.

Evans-Rhydderch, Z. *Mathematics In The School Grounds.* Crediton, Devon, UK: Southgate, 1993.

Feltwell, J. *Beekeeping.* Winchester, Hants, UK: Learning Through Landscapes Trust, 1991.

Keaney, B. *English In The School Grounds.* Crediton, Devon, UK: Southgate, 1993.

Merrick, L. *Land and Water Invertebrates: Identification in the School Grounds.* Crediton, Devon, UK: Southgate, 1993.

Pearce, T. *Exploring Woodlands.* Exeter, UK: Wheaton Education and Hampshire Books, 1990.

Royal Society for Protection of Birds. *Wildlife and the School Environment.* Winchester, Hants, UK: Learning Through Landscapes Trust, 1992.

Thomas, G. *Science In The School Grounds.* Crediton, Devon, UK: Southgate, 1992.

Titman, W. *Special Places, Special People: The Hidden Curriculum of School Grounds.* Surrey, UK: Wild World Fund for Nature/Learning Through Landscapes Trust, 1994.

Young, K. *Learning Through Landscapes: Using School Grounds As an Educational Resource.* Winchester, Hants, UK: Learning Through Landscapes Trust, 1990.

Appendix B

Information Sources and Checklists on Playground Safety

American Society for Testing and Materials (ASTM). *Standard Consumer Safety Performance Specification for Playground Equipment for Public Use*, 1993. 26 pp.
This is a detailed and technical guide for playground equipment and includes definitive standards. It is consistent with the CPSC 1991 *Handbook*. ASTM standards are voluntary, but since they have been agreed to by a wide variety of professional representatives, they have the highest standing in the legal system. If you are planning to review bids for new or renovated equipment and design, these standards will be the benchmarks by which to judge the bids. Order from ASTM, 1916 Race St., Philadelphia, PA 19103-1187; 215-299-5585, Fax 215-977-9679. The cost is $24.15, postage included.

Consumer Federation of America. "Parent Checklist—How Safe Is Your Local Playground?" 1994. 2 pp.
This free, 12-point checklist covers all of the important areas. It's as good for teachers as it is for parents. Not a lot of details but enough to set off alarms. Send a self-addressed stamped envelope to Parent Checklist, Consumer Federation of America, P.O. Box 12099, Washington, DC 20005-0999.

Injury Prevention Research Center. Jambor, T., & S.D. Palmer, *Playground Safety Manual*, 1991. 29 pp.
Cheerfully illustrated, this handbook gives suggestions for keeping maintenance routines and parceling out responsibility for playground safety. Write to the Injury Prevention Research Center, The University of Alabama, Birmingham, AL 35294-2041. The price is $4, postage included. This center also offers a teacher-oriented booklet with checklists that guide you around the play area and help you note what needs to be fixed.

U.S. Consumer Product Safety Commission (CPSC). *Handbook for Public Playground Safety*, 1991.
The authoritative document for overall safety standards, it replaces the 1981 edition and includes standards for preschools as well as for settings for school-age children. It contains a detailed discussion of playground surfaces. Request a free copy from the U.S. Government Printing Office or in writing from "Playground Handbook," Consumer Product Safety Commission, Washington, DC 20207. If you are in a rush, you can call CPSC at 301-504-0580.

Appendix C

Guidelines for Playground Accessibility

(Note: This portion of the guidelines is reprinted here to indicate how specific and careful the requirements are.)

An accessible play area should provide all children with access to the play opportunities which are present. It should also provide opportunities for parents with disabilities to play with their children. At this time, no building codes clearly define accessibility in play areas. While there are many ways in which access can be provided for different play events, the following guidelines identify minimum access requirements for basic play area elements. They have been developed based on the *Play For All Guidelines* and UFAS [Uniform Federal Accessibilty Standards] adapted for children's environments.

A. Access to Play Area

1. Path of Travel (Fig. 1)
To be usable by children with disabilities, an accessible path of travel must be provided into the play area. The path must be smooth, level, stable, and slip-resistant. Stairs may not be used at entries to the area.

2. Access to Equipment
An accessible path of travel must be provided from the entry of the play area to each play activity. This path of travel must meet the following requirements:

a. *Width* (Fig. 2)
Walks must be at least 44" wide to provide access for at least one child using a wheelchair, walker, or crutches. However, 88" is preferable to allow two children using wheelchairs, walkers, or crutches to pass.

b. *Vertical Clearance* (Fig. 3)
Vertical clearance of at least 80" must be provided above walks at all times.

Trees and other overhanging objects must be maintained to provide adequate headroom.

c. *Surfacing*
The walk surface must be safe, firm, and stable (e.g., resilient tiles). Sand, shredded rubber, and wood chips are not acceptable.

d. *Level Changes*
Walking surfaces must be free of level changes that may be caused by tree roots, cracks, or expansion joints. Abrupt level changes are acceptable if they do not exceed ¼". Level changes up to ½" are acceptable if they are beveled with a slope that does not exceed 1:2.

e. *Slope* (Fig. 4)
Walk slope must not exceed 1:20. If a section of walk is steeper, it is considered a ramp and . . . should be completed for that section of the walk.

Reprinted by permission, from S.M. Goltsman, T.A. Gilbert, & S.D. Wohlford, *The Accessibility Checklist: An Evaluation System for Buildings and Outdoor Settings, User's Guide, 2nd Edition.* Berkeley, CA: MIG Communications, 1993), 42-47.
© 1993 by MIG Communications, 1802 Fifth St., Berkeley, CA 94710.

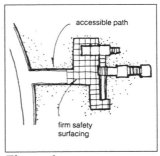

Figure 1

Figure 2

f. Cross Slope (Fig. 5)

Cross slope makes walks hard to navigate for wheelchair users because the chair has a tendency to head down the cross slope rather than straight. Cross slope must not exceed 1:50.

B. Ramps

Since children are the primary users of ramps in play areas, the requirements are stricter than those for typical ramps. For safety reasons, it is recommended that ramps onto play equipment be avoided whenever possible.

1. Slope

Slope of ramps in play areas must not exceed 1:16.

2. Width

Ramps must be at least 44" wide. This is the minimum width required for a child using a wheelchair, walker, or crutches to maneuver.

3. Cross Slope

Cross slope must not exceed 1:50.

4. Drainage

Ramps must be designed so that water will not accumulate on the ramp surface.

5. Slip Resistance

When possible, the surface must be brushed concrete, or a similar surface, to prevent slipping. Due to the weight of concrete, ramps onto play equipment should be constructed of wood or plastic-coated metal.

6. Level Changes

Ramp surfaces must be free of level changes that may be caused by tree roots, cracks, or expansion joints. Abrupt level changes are acceptable if they do not exceed ¼". Level changes up to ½" are acceptable if they are beveled with a maximum slope of 1:2.

7. Ramp Edges

Ramps must include protection from drop-offs at the edges. This can be accomplished with walls, curbs (2" min.), or railings that provide a suitable barrier at the ramp surface (e.g., a continuous rail immediately above ramp surface or vertical railing posts spaced 3" apart as shown in Figure 6). Alternatively, the ramp surface may be widened to extend at least 1 foot past the handrails on each side.

8. Top Landing

The top landing must be 60" by 60" minimum.

9. Bottom Landing

The bottom landing must be at least 60" long and as wide as the ramp (minimum ramp width is 44").

Figure 3

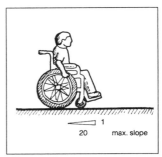

Figure 4

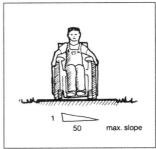

Figure 5

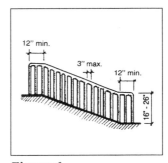

Figure 6

10. Length of Runs
Each run of a ramp must not exceed 12 feet in length.
11. Handrails
Rails are required on both sides of ramps.

a. Railing Size
Round handrails must have a diameter between 1¼" and 1½". Other handrail shapes are allowed if they provide an equivalent gripping surface.

b. Location
Handrails must be exactly 1½" from any adjacent vertical surface.

c. Recessed Handrails
If handrails are recessed into an adjacent surface, the recess must be at least 18" high and no more than 3" deep.

d. Rotation
Handrails must not rotate in their fittings. They should be securely mounted.

e. Surfaces
Handrails and nearby surfaces must be free of sharp edges or burrs.

f. Handrail Ends
Handrails must not end abruptly. They should return to a wall surface, a post, or the ground. Handrail ends may be rounded in lieu of returns. This prevents the possibility of persons inadvertently injuring themselves on an exposed end.

g. Handrail Mounting Height
The top of the rails must be between 16" and 26" above the ramp surface. The desired height within this range varies depending on the age of the predominant user group.

h. Handrail Extensions (Figs. 6 & 7)
Handrails must not end at the top and bottom of ramps. They should extend 12" beyond the ramp, level with the landing surface. This helps children steady themselves when approaching or leaving the ramp. If the ramp provides access onto equipment, the handrails should continue as part of the nonclimbable enclosure.

i. Ramps with Large Rises
If a ramp rises more than 30", a second set of complying handrails must be provided 12" to 16" above the ramp surface.

C. Surfacing Around Equipment
This section must be completed for each individual play area.
1. Surface
The surface must be safe, firm, and stable (e.g., resilient tiles, mats, or poured-in-place

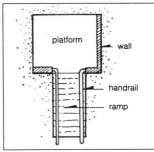

Figure 7

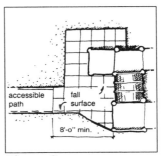

Figure 8

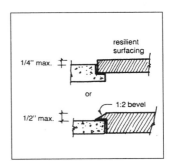

Figure 9

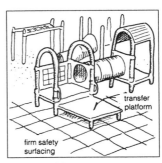

Figure 10

rubber). Sand, shredded rubber, and wood chips are not acceptable.

a. *Type of Surfacing* (Fig. 8)
Resilient surfacing must be provided along the accessible route for areas within 8 feet of equipment. This surfacing must be of appropriate thickness to ensure that a head-first fall from the highest point of adjacent equipment will result in an impact of 200 grams or less. G-force ratings are provided by manufacturers or can be measured with an appropriate testing device.

2. Level Changes (Fig. 9)
Surfaces must be free of level changes that may be caused by tree roots, cracks, or expansion joints. Abrupt level changes are acceptable if they do not exceed ¼". Level changes up to ½" are acceptable if they are beveled with a 1:2 slope.

3. Slope
Slope must not exceed 1:20.

4. Cross Slope
Cross slope makes it hard for children in wheelchairs to navigate because the chair has a tendency to head down the cross slope rather than straight. Cross slope must not exceed 1:50.

D. Play Structures

1. Transfer Platform (Fig. 10)
A transfer platform is one way to access equipment from a wheelchair. It allows a child to transfer between a wheelchair and the play structure. The transfer platform must be on an accessible path of travel.

a. *Clear Space* (Fig. 11)
A 60" by 60" clear level area must be provided on one side of the transfer platform to allow for a front or side transfer.

b. *Parking Space*
For each transfer platform there must be a 30" by 48" space, adjacent to an accessible path of travel, where a child's wheelchair can be left while he or she is on the play structure. This space must be further than 8 feet from the structure to ensure safety.

c. *Size of Transfer Platform*
The platform must be at least 24" by 24".

d. *Height of Transfer Platform* (Fig. 12)
The height of the transfer platform must be between 15" and 17" from the ground.

e. *Handholds* (Figs. 12 & 13)
Handholds help a child maneuver onto the equipment. At least one handhold, positioned 25" to 27" above the ground,

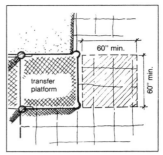

Figure 11

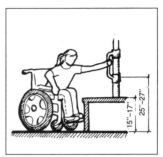

Figure 12

Figure 13

Figure 14

must be provided at the rear of the transfer platform or the transfer platform should have an edge which can be gripped to help a child slide from a wheelchair onto the platform.

2. Deck Surface Material
The deck surfacing material must not cut, scrape, or burn when slid upon.

3. Adjacent Platform Heights
There must be no more than 6" between the transfer platform height and the height of the deck surfaces which lead to the main structure. Because openings between platforms of different heights may trap a child's head or fingers, openings between platforms are not allowed.

4. Grab Bars
Grab bars or handholds must be provided at each level change on the play structure.

5. Vertical Play Walls

a. Equipment Mounting Height (Fig. 14)
Vertical play walls or other equipment which can be used while sitting in a wheelchair must have play events mounted between 20" and 36" above the deck or ground surface. This allows a child in a wheelchair to access the play event from a forward position.

b. Location
Vertical play walls or other accessible equipment must be adjacent to an accessible path of travel.

6. Access to Play Events
All types of play events on the structure must be accessible. This does not mean all play equipment must be accessible, but rather that at least one piece of each type of equipment or play activity is accessible.

E. Sand and Water Trays
This section must be completed for each sand or water tray that is provided in the play area.

1. Surface Height (Fig. 15)
The play surface of the tray must not be more than 30" above the ground surface.

2. Height of Knee Space (Fig. 15)
There must be at least 24" between the ground surface and the underside of the tray.

3. Depth of Knee Space (Fig. 15)
There must be at least 19" of unobstructed space beneath the tray to allow a child in a wheelchair to pull under the tray.

4. Clear Ground Area (Fig. 16)
A level, unobstructed space 30" by 48" min. must be provided at each tray if it is to be usable by a child in a wheelchair.

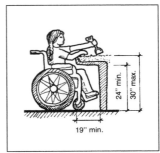

Figure 15

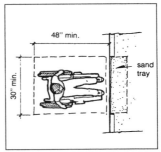

Figure 16

Other resources on accessibility

Blakely, K., M.A. Lang, & R. Hart. *Getting in Touch with Play: Creating Play Environments for Children with Visual Impairments*. New York: Lighthouse for the Blind, 1991. (This has good descriptions of London's playgrounds for children with disabilities.)

Brett, A., R.C. Moore, & E.F. Provenzo, Jr. "Playgrounds and Exceptional Children." Chap. 5 in *The Complete Playground Book*. Syracuse, NY: Syracuse University Press, 1993.

Chandler, P.A. "Preparing Yourself and the Physical Environment." Chap. 3 in *A Place for Me: Including Children With Special Needs in Early Care and Education Settings*. Washington, DC: NAEYC, 1994.

Frost, J.L. "Playgrounds for All Children." Chap. 12 in *Play and Playscapes*. Albany, NY: Delmar, 1992.

Moore, R.C., S.M. Goltsman, & D.S. Iacofano, eds. *Play for All Guidelines, Second Edition: Planning, Design and Management of Outdoor Play Settings for All Children*. Berkeley, CA: MIG Communications, 1992.

Appendix D

IPA and the Declaration of the Child's Right to Play

International Association for the Child's Right to Play (IPA)

IPA is an international, nongovernmental organization [NGO] founded in Denmark in 1961. It is an interdisciplinary organization and embraces in membership persons of all professions working for or with children. The organization works closely with many international NGOs and is recognized by the United Nations Economic and Social Council (ECOSOC) and by UNESCO and UNICEF as a nongovernmental organization with consultative status.

IPA is a human rights organization that shares a feeling of solidarity with children all over the world. IPA endorses the United Nations Convention on the Rights of the Child, particularly Article 31, which states that the child has a right to leisure, play, and participation in cultural and artistic activities. IPA promotes peace education through play and has been appointed as a United Nations Messenger of Peace.

IPA attempts to protect, preserve, and promote children's play as a means of ensuring the *maximum development* of every individual. Play stimulates creativity and the emotional, cognitive, and physical development of the whole child regardless of level of ability. Because children use play to explore their social and physical environment, it is a critical aspect of socialization and environmental education.

IPA members believe that play, along with the basic needs of nutrition, health, shelter, and education, is vital for the development of

This description of IPA, abstracted from IPA's literature, and the IPA Declaration of the Child's Right to Play are reprinted from A. Brett, R.C. Moore, and E.F. Provenzo, Jr., *The Complete Playground Book* (Syracuse, NY: Syracuse University Press, 1993), 179–86, by permission of the publisher. IPA's USA Council Representative is M. Guddemi, Department of Education and Research/KinderCare, 2400 President's Dr., P.O. Box 2151, Montgomery, AL 36102-2151; 334-277-5090.

the potential of all children and the protection and enhancement of their families, cultures, and communities. They believe that participation must be strengthened through play leadership and animation.

IPA members include professionals working in education, design, leisure time facilities, play programming, play leadership training, toys and play materials. Professional development and exchange take place through *Play-Rights*, the IPA quarterly magazine; *Play Journal*, the IPA professional journal; the IPA triennial international conference; regional and national conferences; seminars and study tours; and IPA Resources, London. Membership linkages with action groups in more than forty countries provide for an exchange of ideas and information about innovative, play-related nonformal education programs.

IPA Declaration of the Child's Right to Play

The IPA Declaration of the Child's Right to Play was originally produced in November 1977 at the IPA Malta Consultation held in preparation for the International Year of the Child (1979). It was revised by the IPA International Council in Vienna, September 1982, and Barcelona, September 1989. The IPA Declaration should be read in conjunction with Article 31 of the U.N. Convention on the Rights of the Child (adopted by the General Assembly of the United Nations, November 20, 1989), which states that the child has a right to leisure, play, and participation in cultural and artistic activities.

What Is Play

Children are the foundation of the world's future.
Children have played at all times throughout history in all cultures.

Play, along with the basic needs of nutrition, health, shelter, and education, is vital to develop the potential of all children.
Play is communication and expression, combining thought and action; it gives satisfaction and a feeling of achievement.
Play is instinctive, voluntary, and spontaneous.
Play helps children develop physically, mentally, emotionally, and socially.
Play is a means of learning to live, not a mere passing of time.

Alarming Trends Affecting Childhood

IPA is deeply concerned by a number of alarming trends and their negative impact on children's development:

- Society's indifference to the importance of play
- Over-emphasis on theoretical and academic studies in schools
- Increasing numbers of children living with inadequate provisions for survival and development
- Inadequate environmental planning, which results in a lack of basic amenities, inappropriate housing forms, and poor traffic management
- Increasing commercial exploitation of children, and the deterioration of cultural traditions
- Lack of access for Third World women to basic training in child care and development
- Inadequate preparation of children to cope with life in a rapidly changing society
- Increasing segregation of children in the community
- The increasing numbers of working children, and their unacceptable working conditions
- Constant exposure of children to war, violence, exploitation, and destruction
- Over-emphasis on unhealthy competition and "winning at all costs" in children's sports

Proposals for Action

The following proposals are listed under the names of government departments having a measure of responsibility for children.

Health

Play is essential for the physical and mental health of the child.

- Establish programmes for professionals and parents about the benefits of play from birth onwards.
- Ensure basic conditions (nutrition, sanitation, clean water, and air) which promote the healthy survival and development of all children.
- Incorporate play into community programmes designed to maintain children's physical and mental health.
- Include play as an integral part of all children's environments, including hospitals and other institutional settings.

Education

Play is part of education.

- Provide opportunities for initiative, interaction, creativity, and socialisation through play in formal education systems.
- Include studies of the importance of play and the means of play provision in the training of all professionals and volunteers working with and for children.
- Strengthen play provision in primary schools to enhance learning and to maintain attendance and motivation.
- Reduce the incompatibilities between daily life, work, and education by involving schools and colleges, and by using public buildings for community play programmes.
- Ensure that working children have access to play and learning opportunities outside of the system of formal education.

Welfare

Play is an essential part of family and community life.

- Ensure that play is accepted as an integral part of social development and social care.
- Promote measures that strengthen positive relationships between parents and children.
- Ensure that play is part of community-based services designed to integrate children with physical, mental or emotional disabilities into the community.

- Provide safe play environments that protect children against abduction, sexual abuse, and physical violence.

Leisure

Children need opportunities to play at leisure.

- Provide time, space, materials, natural settings, and programmes with leaders where children may develop a sense of belonging, self-esteem, and enjoyment through play.
- Enable interaction between children and people of all backgrounds and ages in leisure settings.
- Encourage the conservation and use of traditional indigenous games.
- Stop the commercial exploitation of children's play, and the production and sale of war toys and games of violence and destruction.
- Promote the use of co-operative games and fair play for children in sports.
- Provide all children, particularly those with special needs, with access to a diversity of play environments, toys, and play materials through community programmes such as pre-school play groups, toy libraries, and play buses.

Planning

The needs of the child must have priority in the planning of human settlements.

- Ensure that children and young people can participate in making decisions that affect their surroundings and their access to them.
- When planning new, or reorganizing existing developments, recognize the child's small size and limited range of activity.
- Disseminate existing knowledge about play facilities and play programmes to planning professionals and politicians.
- Oppose the building of high-rise housing and provide opportunities to mitigate its detrimental effects on children and families.
- Enable children to move easily about the community by providing safe pedestrian access through urban neighborhoods,

better traffic management, and improved public transportation.
- Increase awareness of the high vulnerability of children living in slum settlements, tenements, and derelict neighborhoods.
- Reserve adequate and appropriate space for play and recreation through statutory provision.

Affirmation

IPA is determined to sustain the momentum created by the International Year of the Child in 1979 to arouse world opinion for the improvement of the life of children and

- Affirms its belief in the United Nations Convention on the Rights of the Child and endorses its belief in Article 31 of the Convention.
- Recognizes that the population of children in developing countries is three-quarters of the world's total child population, and that efforts directed at the promotion of education and literacy, and the stopping of environmental deprivation would improve the capacities of the poorest.
- Affirms its commitment to working with other national and international organizations to ensure basic conditions of survival for all children in order that they may fully develop as human beings.
- Acknowledges that each country is responsible for preparing its own course of public and political action in the light of its culture, climate, and social, political, and economic structure.
- Recognizes that the full participation of the community is essential in planning and developing programmes and services to meet the needs, wishes, and aspirations of children.
- Assures its co-operation with U.N. agencies and other international and national organizations involved with children.
- Appeals to all countries and organizations to take action to counteract the alarming trends which jeopardize children's healthy development and to give high priority to long term programmes designed to ensure for all time the Child's Right to Play.

Appendix E

Organization Resources on the Environment

American Horticultural Society
7931 East Boulevard Dr.
Alexandria, VA 22308-1300
703-768-5700, 800-777-7931; Fax 703-765-6032
Proceedings from a national conference on children's gardens in 1993, organized by the society, form an extremely useful compilation of outstanding garden projects. See "Outdoor Activities" in Appendix A.

The Conservation Fund
1800 North Kent St., Suite 1120
Arlington, VA 22209
703-525-6300; Fax 703-525-4610

Evergreen Foundation
355 Adelaide St. West, Suite 5A
Toronto, Ontario M5V 1S3
CANADA
416-596-1495; Fax 416-596-1443

Florida Advisory Council on Environmental Education
Room 237, Holland Building
Tallahassee, FL 32399-1400
904-487-0123; Fax 904-488-4959

Institute of Ecosystem Studies
Box R, Route 44A
Millbrook, NY 12545-0178
914-677-5343; Fax 914-677-6455

Learning Through Landscapes
Third Floor
Southside Offices
The Law Courts
Winchester, Hampshire
S023 9DL, UK

National Gardening Association
180 Flynn Ave.
Burlington, VT 05401
802-863-1308
Widely recognized for providing both grants of several hundred dollars for projects and a free newsletter.

National Institute for Urban Wildlife
P.O. Box 3015
Shepherdstown, WV 25443

National Wildlife Federation
1440 16th St., N.W.
Washington, DC 20036
202-797-6800

Project H.O.M.E.
(Habitat: Opportunities for Management and Education)
New Hampshire Fish and Game Department
2 Hazen Dr.
Concord, NH 03301

Project Wild
5430 Grosvenor Lane, Suite 230
Bethesda, MD 20814-2142
301-493-5447

Skolans Uterum
(schoolyard enhancement program)
Gareth Lewis
Box 22106
Stockholm S-104 22
SWEDEN

Urban Resource Partnership
Forest Service, USDA
201 14th St., S.W.
P.O. Box 96090
Washington, DC 20090-6090
202-205-1680

Worldwatch Institute
1776 Massachusetts Ave., N.W.
Washington, DC 20036
202-452-1999

WWF UK—World Wide Fund for Nature
Reaching Out (program for teachers)
Education, Panda House
Weyside Park
Goldaming, Surrey
GU7 1XR, UK

> **To share ideas and resources about good school play places, contact this book's author:**
>
> **Mary S. Rivkin**
> Education Department
> University of Maryland Baltimore County
> Baltimore, MD 21228-5398
> 410-455-2383; Fax 410-455-3986
> e-mail rivkin@gl.umbc.edu

First *and foremost, playgrounds should stimulate play, for the values of play are widely documented by researchers and acknowledged by professionals who work with young children. Play is fun, active, spontaneous, self-initiated, and challenging, and it is closely linked to learning and development. The playground is merely a stage where children act out, spontaneously and freely, the events that touch their lives and simultaneously develop durable, resilient bodies through movement. In contrast to bad playgrounds, good playgrounds increase the intensity of play and the range of play behavior. . . . Bad playgrounds limit play behavior, restrict language, reduce physical movement, and create behavior problems.*

Playgrounds should promote learning and development. Play enhances both convergent and divergent problem-solving and it allows better performance on tasks requiring divergent creative thought. Dramatic or symbolic play contributes to a range of developmental virtues including communication, sex-role development, cooperation, perspective-taking ability, creativity, and social and interpersonal problem-solving skills. . . .

The playground should stimulate the senses through a rich array of textures, colors, and forms. It should nurture curiosity through a rich ever-changing environment. Portable materials, growing things, and live animals are the truly flexible materials of a play environment. Portable materials can be used in an unlimited number of play activities; plants change as they grow and with the seasons; animals grow and change, show their personalities, get sick, give birth, eat and drink. The playground should be fun, a place to escape from routine mental fatigue and boredom, a place to relax and enjoy.

The playground should support the child's basic social, physical, and cognitive needs. It should be comfortable, scaled to the child's size, yet physically and intellectually challenging. . . . It should encourage and allow interaction among children, materials, and adults. The environment must be dynamic, providing graduated challenge—and it must be continuously changing. The best playgrounds are never finished.

—Joe L. Frost